MR SIGGIE MORRISON
with his comb and paper

works by Bill Reed
The Pipwink Papers\
Me, the Old Man
Stigmata
Ihe
Crooks
Tusk
Throw her back
Are You Human?
Awash
1001 Lankan Nights book 1
1001 Lankan Nights book 2
Water Workout (Nonfiction)

plays
Burke's Company
Truganinni
The Pecking Order
Mr Siggie Morrison with his Comb and Paper*
The Old Pig Rat
Jack Charles is Up and Fighting
Just Out of Your Ground
You Want It, Don't You, Billy?
I Don't Know What to Do with You!
Paddlesteamer
Cass Butcher Bunting
Bullsh
More Bullsh
Talking to a Mirror
Auntie and the Girl

award-winning short stories *(see title 'Passing Strange')*
Messman on the C.E. Altar
English Expression
The 200-year Old Feet
The Case Inside
Blind Freddie Among the Pickle Jars
The Old Ex-serviceman
Mahood on the Thin Beach
The Shades of You my Dandenong

Bill Reed
MR SIGGIE MORRISON
with his comb and paper

R

This reprint published independently by Reed Independent 2015
Melbourne, Australia

First published under ISBN 0858590263 by Heinemann Educational Australia
Pry Ltd in 1972 in the Australian Theatre Workshop series.

Printed by CreateSpace, an Amazon.com company

Available from Amazon.com, CreateSpace.com, and other retail outlets. Ebook
formats are available from all major online ebook retailers.
paperback: ISBN13-9780994322760
ebook: ISBN13-9780994322777

Re-issue cover: Dilani Priyangika Ranaweera, Dart Lanka Productions,
Colombo, Sri Lanka

National Library of Australia Cataloguing-in-Publication entry
Creator: Reed, Bill, 1939-author.
Title: Mr Siggie Morrison with his Comb and Paper/ Bill Reed.
ISBN: 9780994322760 (paperback)
Subjects: Australian drama.
Dewey Number: A823.3

National Library of Australia Cataloguing-in-Publication entry
Creator: Reed, Bill, 1939-author.
Title: Mr Siggie Morrison with his Comb and Paper/ Bill Reed.
ISBN: 9780994322777 (ebook)
Subjects: Australian drama.
Dewey Number: A823.3

Contents

To broken dreams started by this one,

and to never ends

Introduction

At a time when our playwrights are concerning themselves more with our history than its heritage, it is a startling and exciting experience to be confronted by a new play which is far from the current mainstream in its individuality and perception.

As a director, I was immediately impressed, on the first reading, by the inherent theatricality of the play - the knowledge and understanding of the special requirements that constitute a theatrical event. In this work the combination of knowledge and enquiry gives us not just a play but an experience of the struggle for creation.

The playwright takes us on a journey in search of reality. At times we are totally convinced, (often by use of the unreal theatrical device) at other times we withdraw from these convictions. But our total involvement is governed by the emotions experienced, whether by fake stage characters or real people, so that we are concerned, not just by the search for truth but by man's inhumanity to man. I believe this play has a great deal to say about mankind. Our treatment of each other, whether it be at the humanitarian level of simply helping our fellow man or on the personal level of using and destroying someone for our own gain. Then again it questions our inheritance. Is this the land of milk and honey where the sun continually shines - the land of our fathers where life is wonderful for all men? Is this a great Australian myth?

The Australian theatre is concerning itself with Australian ideas and problems. For me MR SIGGIE MORRISON with his comb and paper is a definite acquisition to this growth, but better still I believe Bill Reed has provided us with a play that is not for our eyes and ears alone but speaks a universal language for all theatres.

Peter Batey, Artistic Director,
South Australian State Theatre Company

1

The Premiere

First performed at Scotch College open-air amphitheatre, Adelaide, by the South Australian Theatre Company as part of the Adelaide Festival of Arts, February 29 1972, with the following cast:

SIGGIE   Neil Curnow
PARSONS   Shawn Gurton
BIG JULIE   Daphne Grey
MISS GLAMORGAN   Rona Coleman
'BOY'   Tony Porter
JARVIS   Brian Wenzel
MISS HOLLAND   Barbara West
MRS PRUFROCK   Julie Hamilton

Directed § designed by Peter Batey

Author's Note: If the cast needs to be reduced for practical purposes, it is suggested that:
1.   JARVIS could very ill-humouredly double up as 'BOY'
2.   BIG JULIE could very disgustedly double up as MISS GLAMORGAN
3.   MISS HOLLAND could very bumblingly double up as MRS PRUFROCK.

One production simply had MISS GLAMORGAN represented by a spotlight on the stage with voice over.

It is suggested that any character changes should be swift and out in the open and with the minimum of change of pace… eg, JARVIS could simply roll up a trouser leg and change voices to take the part of 'BOY'.

The Monologue

The Monologue should be on a continuous tape and run without break from the opening of the doors of the theatre to the closing of the doors of the theatre. It should be piped into both the auditorium and the foyer.

It should be the continuing, organic backdrop to the performance. It is never shut off, but only lowered to an inarticulate, yet still audible level whenever necessary. It is the 'consciousness' of the play, although its effect shouldn't be more than the background 'hum' of, say, other people at an animated gathering

The full text is available on request from the author, but those parts of it given in this playscript can be, in turn, used over-and-over.

When the Monologue 'breaks through' it is as disruptive and of an unknown source to the actors themselves as it is to the audience.

The Monologue Text

You ought to shine through down here. You ought to shine through a little bit more down here. That's what you ought to do. Peek through. There's a hole up there. You could shine through the hole up there a little bit. For a bit. Just for a bit. Let me know you know I'm down here. You ought to know that. You ought to shine through down here just a peek. Now. Please.

I'm cold. I'm wet. I'm cold and wet. I don't want to be cold and wet. I didn't come home to be cold and wet. Don't turn away from me. You oughtn't to turn away from me. Please. Why have you turned away from me? There is a hole up there. You could shine through. There's a hole. You ought to shine through. Why don't you shine through just a little bit? A peek. A little peek There's a hole there. I don't want to die down here. Why should I die down here?

(Coughs)

Smell. Smell. Is it me? It's not me. It's me a little bit. Not all me. You know it's not all me You know I couldn't hold my bowels for days and days. If you shine through a little, just a peek a little bit, you could dry it all up. You could dry it all up. You could dry me up. Bum me. Bum me again. That's what I want. You know that Bum me. That's what I want. It's me. Don't you see? It's me. It's my face. Look at me. It's my face. Don't I shine through it anymore? Don't I? I've come home. It's me, Siggie, and I've come home. I'm home. I didn't come home to die down here. I've come home to you. I came home to you, you know that. You don't shine much in England. You don't shine through much in England, do you?

It's so dark down here. I can't live down here It's too dark for me to live down here. You know that. Why don't you shine through? You could shine through if you wanted to. If you really wanted to, you could shine through just a little bit down here. You should know I've been trying to get back for years. I shouldn't have to be down hem if you're angry with me not coming back. You should have been there and seen what it was like. Not very nice. All that

4

yellow water and all that. Not to mention my arthritis. Which I haven't because I don't want to gripe. What's the use of griping? Griping gets you nowhere because nobody ever listens to you when you're griping. About arthritis in particular. About yellow water in your... in...

(cannot hold back coughing fit any longer)

Nobody wants to know if you've got yellow water in your lungs. Or if you've got arthritis like I've got arthritis. But what can a bloke say? There's nothing a bloke can say about it because nobody even bothers to listen. All they say is stiff. Stiff. That's all you get. Really. Really and truly deep down where it all matters in your mind. That's all you get. Or they've got troubles of their own. When they haven't really because if they had yellow water in their lungs and arthritis of the fingers like I've got and sitting here rotting because I reckon I'm going to rot pretty soon and all itchy and peeing in their trousers like I am, they'd know what trouble really is. I can tell you. I can't even move and it's smelly down here. I can't even turn away from the pong. I know I pong. Nobody has to tell me I pong. Anybody would pong if they were stuck down here like I'm stuck down here not able to even turn away from the pong and it not doing my lungs any good…

Oh, my God Jesus dear sweet Jesus God, help me Please get me out. Please get me out. I don't want to die. Why should I die? Why should I die? I don't want to die. I shouldn't have to die. Why should it be me down here ponging and dying. I've never ever thought about death so why should it be me down here dying when I haven't given death a second thought. Oh, God. Help me. Please help me because I don't want to die. What would the world be like without me? How can I think about dying when the world would be something that didn't have me in it. Something that wouldn't have me in it oh God Jesus sweet dear Jesus. It's blank when I think of death. There's nothing there when I think of death. Why should I be born if all I can do is die because what is the use of living if you're going to die all over the place from the time that you are born. It's not fair. It's not something I asked for. I didn't ask to be down here. I didn't ask to be put down here and to die like this what with all that horrible yellow water in my lungs and Miss Glamorgan.

Miss Glamorgan? Who's Miss Glamorgan? Oh, yeah. Yeah.

Anyway, as I was saying, they say nothing if you try to tell them. What you've got that'd kill anybody else. Nothing. Not a thing. It doesn't matter a thing if I suddenly up with... like that saying; it flows, Siggie, honestly Siggie, it really flows, y'know? if I come up with... just let's say for the sake of, up with...

(outcry; a theatre-wide conversation-stopper)

HELP! HELP! PLEASE... HELP!

What I mean is if I came out with a blood curdler, they wouldn't even... even... they wouldn't even... What's that? Listen! What's that? Ssh. What's that? Let's have a bit of shush...

(but coughs while trying to keep silent.)

Please let the kids come back. I'd be all right if the kids came back. No sweat if the kids came back. I'll play fox. Right, I'll play fox and when they come back they'll think they've done me damage and. I'm not saying they haven't done me a damage. They've certainly done me a damage all right. But when they come back I'll lay down and play possum and they'll think they've done me more damage than even the little bloody... sorry... horrors think they have and they'll have to go and get their daddies or mums or go and get me a policeman. I wonder whether they'll send around the fire brigade. You hear about the fire brigade going and hauling people out of places in the nick of time so it could well be the fire brigade gets around here first. That's if those kids tell them. Even if those kids tell their daddies or their mums or a policeman or anybody. They can tell anybody. I must remember to tell them that. Might make them feel better if they know I don't care whether they tell anybody just as long as they tell someone. After all, it doesn't matter who they tell as long as they tell. That's the main thing. As long as they tell. Not all of them have to tell either. Only one of them has to tell really. Only one of them has to open his mouth. It could be her mouth. Its mouth. That's better. I don't

6

want to be caught being rotten to kids but any kids that do what those kids are doing to me don't deserve proper parents. Things. Things at Christmas time. Books. Though I never had books. But you know what I mean. Any kids who do what they've done to me don't deserve the basic courtesies... good word. Gee, I've got them floating all around my mind. It's incredible... there I go again... how it just comes and goes. All those lovely words. I've always loved all those lovely words. All those lovely words just floating around in your mind just like it's a nice cool pond in a park and all those lovely nice words are swans drifting along and popping out now and again when you last expect it. Don't deserve basic courtesies of common decency... lovely words, those... of a normal society and good friendship and common decencies and nice manners and good behaviour and doing the right things by others when it comes down to it all. Or something or other. You know what I mean.

It's just the stink. It's just the pong. It's just my legs. It's just my leg aching so much and my fingers aching so much and swelling up like they are. Look at them. It's just that all that bubbling in my... you know… lots of places in me really…

(coughs gently by auto suggestion.)

I think I've wet my strides. I think I've done it. I can't help it. I've done it. That's all there. Is to it. I've done it. Not the first time. I've done it. Down there. Oh God, I smell. I smell. Gee, I smell. It smells down. Here and. I've done it in. In my pants. Damn. Damn. Damn. Please. Please. I'm not complaining. No. Not. Complaining. But I. But I think I've done it in my pants. Yes. I think I've done it in my pants. I think I've done it in my pants. What have I done? What is going... to happen...? What's going to happen to me, please? Please?

Mustn't think about it. Mustn't. You mustn't think I'm complaining. It's just that I'm so cold and wet and aching. Well, I was aching and smelly. I just don't like to think I'm doing something down there that I'd be... yes, embarrassed about. Yes, all embarrassed when somebody finds me. When somebody finds me and says what have you been doing down there and then sniffing like they do or me trying to cover up something embarrassing that I've been doing because they wouldn't believe that I've had to do it and there was nowhere else to do it. They don't believe you. That sour looking man. I think it was a man. That sour looking man who was sitting next to me on the plane when I was coming home and asking the nice young air hostess for another seat, he wouldn't believe that I had to do it in one of those lovely brand new brown paper bags. I could tell he wouldn't. Oh, yes. I could tell all right. When I tried to get out excuse me to him each time, he just turned away. He turned away and put his head up in the air. He turned away and put his head up in the air and his nose under one Of those funny old nozzles they had in there where air came through

I didn't care. I was on my way home. I had my ticket in my hand. I would have had my ticket in my hand if they hadn't taken it off me before we got on. That's not the point though. It's as good as having your ticket in your hand when you're sitting in the plane and they haven't turfed you off because if they haven't turfed you off then that means you must have had a ticket in your hand to be able to get on in the first place. Stands to reason. And if you had your ticket in your hand that means you must have been able to buy it. And if they haven't turfed you off and you've been able to buy a ticket then that means you were able to afford to buy the ticket in the first place. That's fair enough. That's logical. Gee, where do I get all these words from? What was it? Never mind.

You would not have thought dear little children could be like that. I was always nice and kind and helpful to dear little children and you wouldn't have thought that dear little children would do a thing like this to me. You'd think they'd care. You'd think they'd say sorry. You'd think they'd go home right away and say: Dad, there's a poor old man stuck down there and what can you do about it. But what can you do about it? There's some little kids who are not dear little children and they're never going to grow up to be nice and kind to old people like me stuck down here like me. Even if they're not stuck down here like me. Dying for all I know. I'm not saying that to scare myself. I don't want to die down here and I know you won't let me die down here but there could be cases of poor old people like me stuck down here or some other place just like this who would die down here if they came across some rotten little kids who didn't care whether they were stuck down here and wouldn't go and tell their daddies or a policeman or get an ambulance or help you out, like. That's what I mean. What I mean is that there are some poor old people who might die down here if they 'were stuck down here like me and they were cold and wet and aching or was aching but now not being able to feel a thing down there which is. Which is just as worse when you think about it because it could be anything. It could be a disease down there in my legs and with a disease down there in their legs like I think there's something wrong with my legs then they mightn't be able to pull out of it if some kids didn't bring them enough to eat even or even go and tell their daddies or mummies. Mummies would be better, because they'd understand...

(*Ed: plus see other monologue bursts given in the play... and on continuous loop*)

ACT I

(Stage dark, except for SIGGIE back stage. He seems to be lying beneath some weight that he has given up trying to shift off him.

He lies statically for a long time, staring up into the spotlight, as though it was the sun. When he speaks it is equally as flatly.

In the meantime, however, the MONOLOGUE continues to dominate the theatre until it gradually decreases into an underlying 'hum'

Finally, SIGGIE finds himself able to be heard... somehow knowing that... and:)

SIGGIE: Who's out there?

(It comes back as an empty echo. In the distance y a dog howls faintly. There is a disturbing and indistinct human cry for attention. An ambulance siren rises then fades again. All this is far off. Nothing more. SIGGIE falls back. The MONOLOGUE bursts through again... quickly, aggressive to him, before receding again suddenly.

The 'sunlight' comes across the old man until it falls directly onto him. He basks in it, until...)

SIGGIE (outcry) *Why've you turned off me?*

(Instantly a blackout, during which the MONOLOGUE hums along with the added background of the ambulance siren receding too.

When the spot returns upon him, he is calm again:)

SIGGIE: I was dreaming... silly... I was here, but it wasn't hurting though and there was a big hall with bouquets of flowers all around me. The sun was shining through the rafters and then this funny shape came in and walked up the aisle towards me. When

10

he came close I saw he was wearing my face and his eyes were closed and I knew he was dreaming and dreaming about me up here and when he woke up I knew, listen, I knew, I would no longer be...

(shudders, then)

Listen, please go and tell your...

(Lighting up.

The 'main stage' set shows half-completed scenery of an airport lounge. At back is a large plate-glass observation window. It is dark outside; only the lights from the control tower shine dimly through.

The actors, except PARSONS, are back stage with SIGGIE being a very loose focal point. MISS GLAMORGAN sits apart from them. They are all carrying scripts to which they will refer occasionally as at an advanced rehearsal. Whenever they do consult these, they speak unmistakably theatrically. Otherwise, they are evidently not 'within' the play.

PARSONS himself is front stage, trouncing up and down, creating 'mentally'.)

MISS HOLLAND: That's all very well.

JARVIS: Why follow anything but your worst nature?

MISS HOLLAND: No, I've arrived where I've got to face my obligations.

JARVIS: You're single.

MRS PRUFROCK: (hotly) So am I. But that doesn't mean to say all single women only have nursed waiters. Worst natures.

JARVIS: Don't you start. I've been through it all myself.

PARSONS: (shout upwards meaning MONOLOGUE) Turn that annoying thing off!

MISS HOLLAND: You haven't got an eighty-year-old mother at home who you've been neglecting for years precisely because your feet have taken you in your own selfish direction.

MRS PRUFROCK: (sententiously) I know. I've been through it all.

MISS HOLLAND: What one's got to be sure of is whether your own thing is a thing worth doing. Oh God, two months and I ache to leave again. Rothenburg, the Tauber, Stuttgart, Konigsberg Klops and strudel and wurst, Berlin. Lieden in the snow on tipsy nights, hic. Mothers… honestly.

MRS PRUFROCK: I was exactly the same.

JARVIS: Ptochocracy!

MISS HOLLAND: What?

JARVIS: Government by beggars. Ptochocratic. This country, this
    (waves script)
archaeological-dig script. It's all so shagging pauce. Tell you what, the best you can hope for back here is to become that single black jelly bean everybody wants in a bag of sucked-out jujubes.

MISS HOLLAND: What worries me is I feel so unreal. Staying imperial somehow when everybody else has... gone metric.

JARVIS: (snorts) Moral émigrés, aren't we all?

MISS HOLLAND: Faites rien. 'Tomorrow's troubles to the windes resolve'.

PARSONS: (flourish at them) Use the time to consolidate, mes enfants. Animate. Behave. Assimilate. Assumizate. Enmesh. Adjunct together.

MISS HOLLAND: (sotto voce, indicating PARSONS) When I told them I was going to work for him, they said he was around the bend. Even in London.

JARVIS: Wagner himself. Raving dead ringer.

MRS PRUFROCK: Oh, let's get on with it. I'd like to go abode wise moi, just for a change.

JARVIS: (joke sniff) I smell the change you mean.

PARSONS: (still acting the creative director) Imbiba mugga fermented mare's milka morning.
    (Stops, starts again)
Co-actate into coagulates. Make more intimated moments magical. Say, a bird flies across the Arctic waste, turns left at the first pole returns across the steppes with a glorious landslide right back to the equator, turns to his mate getting high on monkey juice and says, 'Jesus, that's the real stuff. Have I just been on a freak freeze-out'
    (self rebuke)
Merde, not quite there. Try this:.
    (then)
You are standing on your head looking up at the heavens above you and see the clouds sweeping towards some distant and mysterious white tower. The illusion is that the whole sky is moving and carrying you along with it. But you know it is supposed to the Earth which is moving, so all that empty space out there sky can't be moving per se. But supposing it is just as you think you might be. Are you going to dissolve into it, or it into you? And dissolve how? Into some pinpoint of superheavy mayhems, or into a vast lighthearted dissipation? What we are posing here is: is imagination real thought or visitation?

    (The actors are still gathered around themselves with their scripts, though, and:)

MISS HOLLAND: (looks at script) Where were we?

JARVIS: (reads) 'Night'.

MRS PRUFROCK: (ditto) Day.

JARVIS: Night.

13

MRS PRUFROCK: Pardon poke, day.

JARVIS: It says night, you scarecrow.

MRS PRUFROCK: It says day.

JARVIS: Christ. Night, night.

MRS PRUFROCK: Tell him, dear.

MISS HOLLAND: Well... dayish. I suppose. It varies at the turnarounds, you know.

> *(By now, PARSONS has regathered his creative juices. He looks down, then around, then with right theatrical mood caught, drops to his knees and knocks   on the floor boards.)*

PARSONS: We know you're there, Siggie. Somewhere down there among the... not to put too much of a pretty picture on it... the rats. Slugs. Earwigs. What have you. Backing your skinny arms against the slimy wet walls.

> *(BIG JULIE strides in behind PARSONS and cuts them all off. She goes up to the others and points to where, back stage, SIGGIE in his technicolour Sunday-best outfit -- but trousers too big and coat shroudish -- staggers under the weight of a cheap cardboard suitcase from left and eventually off right. PARSONS doesn't notice him, nor the actors being led off in disgust by BIG JULIE.)*

PARSONS: Siggie? Come on, Siggie. Stale urine raising steam. Smelling yourself. Alas, Siggie, mate, who hasn't piddled in his pants some time in his life? Keeps you from drying up. Know what I mean?
     (pause)
What're you thinking, Siggie? Oysters for breakfast? Out of bed, p.m. The old one-two shuffle with cane and monocle, Astaire twirl of the old duke and away he goes... Siggie Morrison, bon viveur, life's traveller... England, Europe, Siam, Warrnambool... Siggie Himself swanking down Castlereagh Street. We're all turning our

heads. Who's the pop Pop? Who's the dandy Daddy? The cry goes up. Siggie Morrison, who else, you dead ignoramuses. Or ignorami. Siggie's arrived back in Australia at last. Honky tonk. The harbour bridge falls into the sea. Members of all parliaments confess to being boy scouts. Come on, Siggie. Relent.

(BIG JULIE re-enters, stands looking down at PARSONS with contempt. He senses her presence, looks up, laughs nervously.)

BIG JULIE: Now I've seen it all.

PARSONS: (knocks on the stage boards) Sydney. Down here.

BIG JULIE: Oh, yes.

PARSONS: Why not? I make it Sydney. I dub thee Sydney of the Southern Cistern Seas.

BIG JULIE: You need dubbing on your deadwood.

PARSONS: I was using the divine human attribute of abstract reconstruction.

BIG JULIE: (eyes upward) Good God.

PARSONS: I will ignore that by pointing out that if mere prop men, at a few right-hand turns of a few countersunk screws, are able to string a few bits of wood together and say, right, This is an airport lounge. No, more. London airport. And if you don't believe it, then up yours. Now if yer actual tradesmen can shove that down yer gullet, I say: All right, I, being the leading creative light around here... I say it modestly... I wish to add to all this: fine, and Sydney's down here and old Siggie's down here and if you laugh at that, and don't give me any of your sneering hiccoughs, you're in the wrong game. That's all. Signing off.

BIG JULIE: Ha. Ha.

PARSONS: I'll ignore that too. Visions sharpened by the fourth dimension. I, an actor... an ancient craftsman looming away at his dying art... adding for my own amusement... although admitting that that need not negate the inherent flair of it all... a bird, for example, with its wings clipped is still inherently capable of flying... I may be quoted... as I, an actor without spectators am still capable of shooting a certain style, shall we say, at blank spaces... adding, to re-iterate, a qualm of a soupcon, a pinch of imagination's adumbration... look it up in the online Oxford... to the dreary and unchanging three dimensions of wood and plaster board...

(BIG JULIE burps loudly.)

PARSONS: (pained) That is extremely rude. Still, I say again. This is the northern airport from which Siggie Morrison, hero of our play, journeys home after forty years. Creative statement. Siggie Morrison after forty years is travelling Down Under. Ergo.
     (knocks on floor boards)
This way in the mind's eye. Down here, therefore, is Sydney. There. You may not realize it, but I have just retrieved your sense of logic through illusion. You needn't thank me. I shall go even further.
     (knocks on the floor boards again)
Listen. If you tap Sydney, it's hollow too.

BIG JULIE: Like your head.

PARSONS: (calls out) Take five.

BIG JULIE: We're taking more than five. We've gone on strike, tinkerbell.

(And turns to go off.)

PARSONS: No, seriously. Imagine if Siggie Morrison was a real person, renamed only for the exigencies of drama. Imagine him stepping arthritically out of some room-and- board right now in his yellow corduroy pants and his pink shirt and his white straw hat, carrying that ridiculous lady's mauve umbrella... started out on his daily circuit with the snot drop hanging from the end of his nose and his little reptilian eyes filling up with decrepit pools while, behind, the landlord tries to think of ways he can get the little drip out of the room... and some hairy labourer right now is pointing out that little technicolour poof to his mates... If that's what a flesh-and-slosh Siggie Morrison was probably doing right now... actual, breathing, material and murmuring his idiotic little 'my, my's' and 'geez's' to all the retrorockets in women's ears... then for the sake of argument, this...

(taps boards)

'ere be Sydney. And down there, Siggie Morrison crawls away into his sad, pathetic tear-jerking existence just as really as if he was up on the stage here with us right now...

(Before huffing off, BIG JULIE disgustedly turns PARSONS' head around so that he can see SIGGIE back onto stage dragging his suitcase along the ground, sighing, letting the suitcase drop, catching his breathy then speaking back to the wings.)

SIGGIE: Crikey me, of course I will. I'll just wait here. Don't you all go worrying about little old me.

(He smiles warily at PARSONS. Then notices the couch and, dragging his suitcase after, goes over to it, lies back with eyes closed.

PARSONS turns away when he recovers his senses, tries to ignore SIGGIE's presence... whistles, sits, examines a bit of prop, calls for coffee -- nobody answers -- examines his fingernails until he cannot stand it anymore. Whips around to SIGGIE)

PARSONS: What's the game?

SIGGIE: Sorry, this your seat?

PARSONS: Never mind about the seat.

SIGGIE: I didn't mean to take your seat.

PARSONS: I don't care about the seat.

SIGGIE: I wouldn't like to have taken your seat.

PARSONS: Forget the seat!

SIGGIE: You don't come across somebody nice enough to give an old man like me his seat often. Not these days.

PARSONS: (into air) Big Julie!

BIG JULIE: (head appears) Don't call me Big.

PARSONS: Julie!

BIG JULIE: (reappears, indicates SIGGIE) Answer that then, divine re-creator.

>	*(retracts head again)*

PARSONS: Big Julie! Julie!

>	*(no reply)*

SIGGIE: My, my. I'm all so excited.
	(giggles)
It's the first time I've ever flown. It's the first time I've ever flown through clouds, too. I've always wanted to fly through those lovely clouds. They say it's like snow. But it's vapour really. That's where we get the word vapourized from. From flying through clouds that we think are like snow. Excuse me.

>	*(He closes his eyes again.)*

PARSONS: You!

SIGGIE: Oh dear. My friends said it'd be all right for me to wait here on this seat.

PARSONS: (suspiciously) What friends?

SIGGIE: They came all the way up to see me off. Isn't that nice? I'm going home.
	(Giggles)
I've been away forty years give or take. I'm an Australian.

PARSONS: All the world's a stage Australian.

SIGGIE: Forty years, two months and three days.
    (giggles)
Stayed Aussie all that time even if I say so meself.

(And closes his eyes again.

PARSONS hurries over to the wings.)

PARSONS: (off) How did he get here?

BIG JULIE: (head on) I found him in the Mens, if you must know.

PARSONS: In the Men's can?

BIG JULIE: (defiantly) I've got nothing to hide.

PARSONS: Don't you know who he's trying to impersonate?

BIG JULIE: Give over. Who else could look like that? Bit of luck the poor old bugger has brought his lawyer along to sort you out too.

PARSONS: (reverting to style) Mere bagatelle of an imbroglio. Main street, rush hour, two people suddenly dash into each other's arms, make violent love by the fire hydrant. They don't know each other's name. It's just that for the last twenty years they've just bumped into each other on the way from work and had it away by the fire hydrant. That's imbroglio. Who's to blame?
    (to 'off')
Did someone take that down? We might be able to use it later.
    (back to BIG JULIE)
However, imbroglio must be in good taste before I'll go along with it.
    (indicating SIGGIE)
That ain't good taste.

SIGGIE: (looking up) If you see my friends, would you tell them I'm here? Case I go the nod off, you see.

19

(They stop. But SIGGIE says no more. Finally...)

PARSONS: I warn you. I shall maintain my aloof stance against ridiculous imported possibilities.

BIG JULIE: You should have seen your slack gob when old Siggie walked on, big man.

PARSONS: (carefully) Who said it's Siggie?

BIG JULIE: I asked him, you squashed dung.

PARSONS: (uncomfortable nonchalance) How can it be Siggie? There's no Siggie up here. He lives with Charon in men's minds down beneath the aspidistra roots.

BIG JULIE: Like hell there ain't no Siggie, you shiver of shot.

PARSONS: I wouldn't pull a thing like that on an old man who was real.

BIG JULIE: Yeah, you'll kick yourself all the way to the bank.

PARSONS: Art and association.

BIG JULIE: Bad art and bank accounts, you mean. You conned your way around him. They give them free legal aid these days.

PARSONS: (shivers) Don't say things like that.

BIG JULIE: I always knew about you. But this is where you really strained your striber with me.

PARSONS: (whisper) Is he asleep?

BIG JULIE: No, he's just working up the energy to get at your jugular. And that's in your damn pocket, too...

PARSONS: (generally) Everybody hold everything! Hold it! We'll start again. And this time let's work together to arrive at something, given that the moment of infant rift from the mother has come to us all.

(clicks finger at SIGGIE)
Go away.

(Waits but nothing happens.)

BIG JULIE: You stand to make a bomb out of this damn play.

PARSONS: (evasively) Where's the others?

BIG JULIE: Looking at you, thinking what a tic you are. We didn't know he even existed. You're just psycho enough to make up something like him. You didn't even bother to change his name. Mongrel.

PARSONS: Typical feminine reaction.

BIG JULIE: You... crossbreed.

PARSONS: I deny that. Anyway, assume with great assumption that this really is Siggie. I would have done him a favour by using his name. I nestled him within the diphthongs of my art... pupated him... gave him a cocoon to you... Siggie Morrison, the pupa Poppa. Dozing in a nice quiet sunny corner of the theatrical garden. What's wrong with that?

(BIG JULIE burps at him again. PARSONS indicates SIGGIE.)

PARSONS: I ask you: who is this... screw-on screwdriver anyway? Another secret of your whoreabouts?

BIG JULIE: (shrugs) Use the spare flair of your imagination. Your two backs are showing.

(She goes off.)

PARSONS: (after her) And you need a lifesaver to take up the slack.

BIG JULIE: (comes back on, grabs him by shirt front) Look, you...

PARSONS: Beat me. I'm suffering already.

(BIG JULIE releases him in disgust, goes off. PARSONS turns to SIGGIE, watches as the sunlight from outside slowly pans across to fall across SIGGIE. As it strikes him, he comes awake with a delighted cry, gets up to stand in its warmth. Tries to 'dry out'.

SIGGIE and the MONOLOGUE start up saying the same thing together as he does so. At first his ululating of the sunshine has him audible with the MONONLOGUE but he is soon merely mouthing what it is saying, and even sooner not bothering to try to keep up with it anyway)

MONOLOGUE and SIGGIE initially: (all around) I was born in the sun. I don't like not being in the sun. I always said to myself, I said: it's not right not being in my sun.

PARSONS: (to wings) What about a bit of help back there?

MONOLOGUE and fading SIGGIE: (all around) Come over here, Siggie, they said. Come back home. We know a place where your sun, where you, where your sun shines through all day every day. Where you never miss a beat, they said. They said a place where you shine through all the time, summer, winter, autumn and that other time. Spring, that's it. Spring. Fancy me forgetting Spring. They said it made no diff. Summer, autumn, winter or spring. They said. Because you shine through all day every day, see, Siggie. Even all night if you want, every night. Although I didn't believe that … I mean fancy expecting a man to believe that. Every day and all day. My sun. Well, why not? Where there's a lemon-scented hum and a salmon gum and there's a poplar popping up all over the place and a bloom, like, and there's…

PARSONS: (above fading MONOLOGUE) Anyway, let's not jump to conclusions. It might be him, then again it mightn't be him. Let's put it this way: it could be him but it ought not to be him. All I can do is grant you a certain ambience, that's all. And to be perfectly crude, ambience sucks.

(The MONOLOGUE resides to its normal background humming.

PARSONS stares daggers up at the control room.)

SIGGIE: (up at sunlight) You don't shine through much anymore. I'm cold and wet. I'm in pain... somewhere...
     (confused)
it's wet and slimy in here... pain somewhere...

PARSONS: I'm in pain. We're all in bloody pain. Go on, get it off your convex chest. Say you remember me. Say I remind you of someone. I can't stand people... standing around.

SIGGIE: (sweetly) Are you from the airline? How nice.
     (giggles)
I had to take all sorts of odd jobs to save up my fare. But I finally made it. Heavens, I'm not boring you, am I? You will say if I'm boring you, won't you? Don't feel you've got to keep me company just because you're from the airline people, because I always bore people like airline people.

PARSONS: You won't bore me.

SIGGIE: But you will tell me if I bore you, won't you? Promise?

PARSONS: (bored) I'll tell you if you bore me.

SIGGIE: The awful thing is I know I'll bore you sooner or later. My, everybody's being so nice to me. Last year, I cleaned up a bank for a bit. The back manager left me a note one night. ... Have I told you this?

PARSONS: (still bored) His note read: 'Dear Mr Morrison, you don't seem to be able to remember any of the little notes I leave behind for you, so I'm afraid we'll have to let you go'...
     (as much as he can round on the old man)
1 know all about it but where did you get it from?

SIGGIE: I think it was under his Dictaphone thingo.
     (giggles)

23

Knock, knock.

PARSONS: Who's there?

SIGGIE: Dictaphone.

PARSONS: Dictaphone who?

SIGGIE: (giggles) Dictaphone up your... (stops, shivers.) Why is it so cold and wet and slimy here...? It's getting at... my pain... somewhere.

PARSONS: You're not cold and wet and slimy.

SIGGIE:- I feel cold and wet and slimy. My old legs feel heavy.
    (sits)
It's not right never to have my sun, is it? White things without blood crawl around under tin when the sun doesn't shine...
    (he stops, convulsively brushes revolting things off his legs.)
Uh.

PARSONS: For shit's sake, don't have a fit on me.

SIGGIE: Mushrooms growing. Yellow thingmebobs when I cough. Yellow water in my lungs. I'd never eat mushrooms...
    (then directly up at PARSONS)
Would you eat mushrooms?

PARSONS: I'd eat off an overcrowded fly screen. Now please go. Leave the snothouse without leaving too much snot.

SIGGIE: Without the sun, I wouldn't have grown. Truly. Not that silly old me is anything. Blood oath, no. But what sort of world would it be without me? Gee, I'd be something that *wouldn't be in it.*
    (shudders)
I was born in the sun. In the back of my dad's ute on the way to hospital. I think. That was in Australia. I am Australian. You mightn't wear that, but I am. They wouldn't believe me.

MONOLOGUE: (sudden burst) They said, Siggie come with us. I said why I don't mind telling you. I said why all suspicious like. But I didn't like to let somebody know you're all suspicious. It doesn't help relationships if you let somebody know you're all suspicious. They go and get all suspicious if they think you are being suspicious. They think hello what's he or she been doing to make me feel suspicious that he's feeling suspicious about me. It's the insinuation. Beaut word that. I say again. What was that...

> *(stops as suddenly as it begun but it has been enough to have SIGGIE covering his ears and rebelling against it)*

SIGGIE: (trying to get above it) *They wouldn't believe a man!*

PARSONS: (shouting too) Who?

SIGGIE: (agitated) Kids... jumping about on the tin sheets on me...!

> *(Long pause, until:)*

PARSONS: You would turn up sooner or later, wouldn't you?

SIGGIE: I'll just rest here until my friends come back.

> *(PARSONS indicates his annoyance by coming forward and yelling up at the theatre's control room at the back of the auditorium)*

PARSONS: Testing, testing. One, two, three...

> *(Listens, gets no acknowledgment, shrugs, turns away.)*

SIGGIE: (conversationally) Are you going on the same plane? I hope you won't give me tomato sandwiches. I wouldn't even dare go in a lift with a tomato sandwich under my belt.
    (giggles)
Who wants more wind up there?
    (then)
Are you going home too?

25

PARSONS: Strike me lucky.

SIGGIE: (delighted) Roy Rene Mo.

PARSONS: (mimic of Mo) No, no. So help me, I'm a dirty great spud on top of a lot of flaming matchsticks... call a mug mash-head.

SIGGIE: I could tell you were Australian too. What've you been doing over here?

PARSONS (now pretty much looking for help) I'll bite… where?

SIGGIE: London. Gawd. Whatareya?

PARSONS: (stops, looking about) Oh... London.

SIGGIE: London.

PARSONS: London... oh, sure.
    (looks at him closely, then runs excitedly towards wings, speaks off.)
He really thinks he's still in London!

BIG JULIE: We could have told you that half an hour ago.

PARSONS: (accusingly) Put-up job.

BIG JULIE: Sure, sure.

PARSONS: (decision) Nobody do anything. I've got to think.

BIG JULIE: Yeah and that way, *you* get to do nothing.

PARSONS: (to wings) As I see it there are three alternatives. All of which aren't worth a pig's arse, I admit. However...
    (back to SIGGIE)
Actually, it was dictaphone up your directory. Or dictionary.
    (then back to wings)
Okay, so we shut down. We shall inertia-ize rather than anathematize... look that up in your English aids to Australian

26

actors... him out. We shall sit around him and *stare*. Bodily. Sedentary as the seasons in slide shows. Note the attachment of words to the various alloyed anodes around which art bubbles. He will then fidget; we will do nothing. He will ask perhaps for a script; we will do nothing. Eventually he will ask for the bus fare. I myself am broke, but one of you will...

(MISS GLAMORGAN skips onto the stage from the other side to the accompaniment of an extract from 'Swan Lake'. She is dressed in a long white robe, with a white rose in her hair, and is bathed in a sweet and pure light.)

MISS GLAMORGAN:
Awake! for Morning in the Bowl of Night
Has flung the Stone that puts the Stars to Flight
And Lo!...

PARSONS: Abort, abort!

(PARSONS grabs MISS GLAMORGAN, tries to muffle her. She struggles, strangely trying to make it over to SIGGIE)

PARSONS: What the.. Miss Glamorgan!

SIGGIE: (sits bolt upright, into air) Miss Glamorgan?

MISS GLAMORGAN: (directed at SIGGIE) Yes!

(But is shoved off, muffled.)

SIGGIE: Did somebody say Miss Glamorgan?

PARSONS: (innocently) Miss Glamorgan?

SIGGIE: Somebody said Miss Glamorgan.

PARSONS: You said Miss Glamorgan.

SIGGIE: (really distressed) I thought somebody was saying Miss Glamorgan.

PARSONS: Oh, her.

SIGGIE: Who?

PARSONS: Her.

SIGGIE: What 'her', please?

PARSONS: (viciously) Miss Glamorgan.

SIGGIE: (thinks, then giggles) Leg puller, you.

PARSONS: (testing him out) Granted later in life than most but your cart-horse of love. That Strabo of your purse-strings. Miss Glamorgan. Right?

SIGGIE: (laughs weakly) I don't think it could have been. Poor Miss Glamorgan died years ago. How did you know about Miss Glamorgan?

PARSONS: (testing again) All right, I'll come clean. It was an actress playing Miss Glamorgan.

SIGGIE: (distressed) Oh dear, have I done something wrong? Why would anyone want to do that to poor Miss Glamorgan?

PARSONS: Nothing's hidden from the director's script, dad.

SIGGIE: Is that like a print-out?

PARSONS: Exactly..

SIGGIE: (nodding sadly) Nothing.

PARSONS: Ah yes, inevitably, the hot breath of the great blanking-off beginning to warm the back of your neck, old chum, a believer in the ancient occult. 'On occult of my old age'. In all the heavenly ladies' bodies, eh?

(SIGGIE giggles.)

PARSONS: Well now, shall we prophesy where you are now, or tell you where you were or conflute... conflute?... conflute, of my own manufacture, where you're going to. And to what, of your own manufacture.

SIGGIE: (impressed) Geez...

PARSONS: Service, service. To the great meeting hall of life and its ha-ha sick joke pitfalls.
     (grabs SIGGIE's hand)
Aha.

SIGGIE: Aha?

PARSONS: What we in the art-of-magic trade call the inside itch. This dandy Rio Grande of a handy is the cosmic arrival-at of *(a)* a musician, *(b)* an effeminized actor, *(c)* an action painter, *(d)* a beautician... or *(e)* a compassionate dog-catcher. You are neither. So much for theory.

SIGGIE: (wonder at one hand) Is that all down on there?

PARSONS: Lithographically etched. Call me the gypsy who doesn't palms empty as the Sahara, Blue.

> *('PARSONS turns away but with hand out for coin, busker-wise. While SIGGIE fumbles for some money and finally holds it pleadingly out, the actors, dressed for the street, walk across back stage.*
>
> *They catch PARSONS out trying to get money from SIGGIE and their conversation is a la behind-the-arras, although, apart from BIG JULIE, they don't care all that much. Their conversations are 'under' the attempted fleecing of SIGGIE by PARSONS and are:*

BIG JULIE (at PARSONS) Hey!
     (to others)
He's even fleecing him now. What a bozo!

MISS HOLLAND: He's all woolly and greasy?

29

BIG JULIE: Lifting his money off him.

MISS HOLLAND: He wouldn't.

BIG JULIE: Wouldn't he?

MISS HOLLAND: He's doing it again.

JARVIS: The dog bit me for five just now too. Can you beat it?

MRS PRUFROCK: I don't know about you lot. Me, I'm going back to flamish my new flurt. Flat. Furnish it.

(Meanwhile ☺

SIGGIE What else do you see, Mr Gypsy?

PARSONS (finding a few more coins) I really shouldn't.

SIGGIE C'arn.

PARSONS You insist on twisting my arm?
(grabs the old man's palm again)
Well, so happens I do see the mount on Queen Moon if you insist on being a believer. The small lines leading to her, here and here. They signpost vast journeys of the mind. Real rambles among the brambles, like.

SIGGIE: (giggles) I forget things.

PARSONS: The pronounced volcano of the Great Sun God.

SIGGIE: I think that's my old boil.

PARSONS: I see a journey of the mind.

SIGGIE: (wonder) That right?

PARSONS: Great eruptions of the orb of day.
(At 'BOY' who is with the others)
Get ready, kid!

30

MISS HOLLAND: (at 'BOY'; Don't you dare.

> *(PARSONS conducts behind SIGGIE's back. Sun music rises, takes over even from the MONOLOGUE, lights dim allowing a sort of sunlight down a storm water drain to fall on SIGGIE. He rises adoringly to it. 'BOY' throws himself into a mime.*
>
> *The actors watch as the 'BOY' goes through his rehearsed paces.)*

PARSONS: Now, listen to the past's metaphysical stirring as though you were lying next to some drunken old lover... Yesterday is alive and well, caught forever in the slipstream of rumour and percussion.

SIGGIE: (hissing) I didn't think they'd find me in time.

PARSONS: Well, if you must be prosaic about it.

SIGGIE: I didn't think they'd ever find me.

PARSONS: (shrugs) Okay.
    (then)
The boy thinks the old man he's discovered down the storm water drain is going to die. The sun scorching down on his piebald prebald pate.

SIGGIE: On the back of my neck, really.

PARSONS: Lost in a hot and open land. Crying out, before he learnt how to swear...

SIGGIE: Cripes!

'BOY': Hey, hey, oldie!

PARSONS: A million suns dancing milleniumously... my word so we'll let it stand.. behind his awful oozing orbs.

'BOY': Howsitgoin'?

31

PARSONS: Up there where the boy is, it looks to Siggie like leaves are autocombusting by his young face. The great fire god exploding triumphs in the swirls of his imagination.

SIGGIE: (outcry to sunlight) My life!

(Drain sunlight immediately off SIGGIE. Sun music fades.)

PARSONS: The heat, the sun, the whole gamma ray bit, obliterating everything. Memory, inquiry, passions, ambition, common dee-eff, verve. Everything. All so much evaporation for the unquenchable furnace of the sun.
(viciously)
And you left with a few wits and a few gristly sinews to embroider the few dry mind grains left behind. Siggie Morrison, dimmed dim wit. And all because the sun, your sun, chose you out of something like the six billion inhabitants of the world to alight upon.- Right?

SIGGIE: (hiss) Yes.

PARSONS: (pulls out a paper party horn and blows it) What a crapload of excrescence.

SIGGIE: (heedless) My father said, I was never the same again after the sun got at me when I was knee-high to a grasshopper. That's why I couldn't remember things anymore and I know it made me a bit funny.
(then)
Hailey's Comet caused it all, you know.

PARSONS: Go on.

SIGGIE: Nineteen hundred and ten. Not only me. It got at Paris, too. It flooded Paris. King Edward the Seventh was lying in state in Westminster. That's what it did. People said something would happen after Edward the Seventh died. It was just unfortunate it happened to me.
(giggles)
Did you see that dopey little kid mucking around me just then?

PARSONS (coyly) What dopey little kid?

32

SIGGIE Cheeky little b.

MISS HOLLAND (back still with the rest of the cast) He's a
little doll really, don't you think? Pity about the baldness.

BIG JULIE What's bald got to do with it. I've had baldies who'd
put the rest of them to shame. Take Jarvis here.

JARVIS (outraged) No going on about baldies when a man's got
a wig on! What's the bloody theatre coming to.

BIG JULIE What're you on about? *Christ.*

> *(But real chimes for an airport announcement stop them
> short, bring their attention back to the real presence of
> SIGGIE)*

ANNOUNCEMENT: 'British Airways announces the departure
of Flight 375 to the Bahamas, stopping at New York. Would
passengers kindly proceed to Gate number five for their boarding
passes...

> *(fades.)*

SIGGIE: Where did they say?

PARSONS: (genuinely) Who?

MISS HOLLAND: (quite irreverently) I didn't mean baldies
can't be funny, you know.

> *(But the others are concentrating on PARSONS and
> SIGGIE now)*

SIGGIE: They said British Airways, didn't they?
    (searching)
I think I'm Qantas. They didn't say anything about Qantas, did
they? Cripes nobody said anything about the Bahamas? Where's
the Bahamas? Geez, I don't know where my ticket's gone. They
said it's all on my ticket. Now I've lost my ticket.
    (at PARSONS)

33

Hey, mister, you seen my ticket lying about? Have you seen any of my friends asking for a bloke?

PARSONS: (daggers at actors) Don't count on friends. They've got tickets on themselves.

SIGGIE: (looking off) They should've come back by now. I think one of them has my ticket. How can I go if I haven't got my ticket?

PARSONS: You haven't got any ticket.

SIGGIE: I can't go without my ticket. Help me please? I think I've lost my ticket.

PARSONS: (angrily) No ticket.

SIGGIE: (appalled) Don't tell me I've lost my ticket now.

PARSONS: You won't believe me when I tell you no ticket?

SIGGIE: Where'd a man be without his ticket?

PARSONS: Okay have it your way. Look again. Strip search yourself. While the world edges towards its inevitable calamity, stay here rooted to the spot looking for a ticket.

> *(SIGGIE starts all over again looking for his ticket, while the cast have another of their side-conversations again;*

MISS HOLLAND: Aw, look at the poor little thing.

JARVIS (but not moving) They won't let him on any plane. I can smell him from here. Me, I'm taking off.

MISS HOLLAND: Do you think we should leave him here just like that?. He's getting a bit het up, poor old man.

JARVIS: He'll be all right.

MISS GLAMORGAN: He won't be all right. That Parsons keeps shouting at him.

JARVIS: Here she's going to go again.

MISS GLAMORGAN: (calls) Mr Morrison.

JARVIS: So go and mother him.

MISS GLAMORGAN: (rebuked, hotly) You had a mother! Mr Morrison probably never had a mother!

> *(MISS GLAMORGAN runs off, but soon sheepishly returns.)*

JARVIS: (after her) He probably came out of your body too.

BIG JULIE: The best thing for us to do is get the hell out of here and leave Parsons holding the baby.

> *(They go to leave.)*

PARSONS: (but short-circuits them) Excuse me, but before you desert, scuttle over here and listen to this.
　　(the actors draw near)
Right, ladies and luggers, I have called you together to hear this. (Turns to SIGGIE.) Old man, for the tenth time, no ticket. You've just stumbled into the right place, old cock. See, the trouble is, they've bounced you around so much in your sorry existence that you obviously don't know whether you're Billy or Martha Graham. Sydney here and now. London you left years ago. If you ever left, which I will grant was most likely. So listen carefully old sonofagun…
　　(into SIGGIE's ear)
no ticket!

SIGGIE: (panic) Please… is there somewhere to go to when you've lost your ticket? It's just that I seem to have lost my ticket, see.

PARSONS: No damn ticket!

SIGGIE: I know it was in my wallet. I had it in my wallet. Now I can't find my ticket.

PARSONS: No wallet!

> *(But SIGGIE pulls out a wallet)*

> *(PARSONS grabs SIGGIE's wallet. A ticket flutters to the ground. SIGGIE swoops delightedly.)*

SIGGIE: I knew I'd put it in my wallet. Geez, don't I ever get het up over nothing sometimes.

PARSONS: (looking at ticket) Cheap forgery.

SIGGIE: (grabs it, to it) Where're you been you little buggerlugs?

MISS HOLLAND (aside to actors) I told you we shouldn't just leave him here, all het up like that.

JARVIS He'll outsurvive the cockroaches, this one.

MISS GLAMORGAN: (hotly returning) I heard that. You shouldn't talk to him like that.
    (mainly at PARSONS)
Shouting at him all the time like that.

JARVIS: (re MISS GLAMORGAN) I told you she'd go off again. Somebody get a good leg thrown over her.

MISS GLAMORGAN: (calls) Mr Morrison.

JARVIS: So go and mother him.

MISS GLAMORGAN: (rebuked, hotly) You had a mother! Mr Morrison probably never had a mother!

> *(MISS GLAMORGAN runs off yet again only to sheepishly return as before and probably for the thousandth time.)*

JARVIS: (after her) He probably came out of your body too.

36

BIG JULIE: You've said that. Now just shut it!

PARSONS: So, old fellah, whatcha reckon? You see where we are here

SIGGIE: Pardon?

PARSONS: No London. No Bahamas. Find any money when you found that wallet, did you?

SIGGIE Eh?

BIG JULIE: (at PARSONS) Big shot. You couldn't flash your way out of a nudist colony.

PARSONS: (ignoring her) To put it bluntly, Siggie old sausage, your providing brain and your sustaining nerves, as they say, are out of whack. So you stumble into an abstraction...
    (waves arm generally)
this... and cuddle it longingly, nostalgically, to your negative nipples. I don't know, perhaps you think you're halfway through your second bottle of metho. I purely surmise that, so never mind. All of us here have known the quiet madness and sadness and badness. No pubescence without the pubes. But go back, old man. Go back to your YMCA cubicle or whatever and dream. There's no law against dreams. Dreams are stuffs; be satisfied with that. We'll see you right. Who knows, if the box office rolls its lovely rolls, you might be able to go back to England. Now can I be fairer?
    (silence)
In short, old gutzer, leave it to the professionals, what say? See, right now, we're supposed to be working. You'll just hate yourself in the morning if you cause an industrial dispute.

> *(He sits back. They all do. Long fidgety pause, during which SIGGIE keeps glancing at the lounge 'entrance ' and they at him.*
>
> *Finally, to break the impasse, PARSONS takes charge again...)*

PARSONS: All right, for the sake of a tear drop on a burnt leaf, we'll call him Sigmund Morrison.

SIGGIE: (giggles) Make it Siggie among friends.

BIG JULIE: (at PARSONS) And?

PARSONS: Admitting playfully that this play might then be based, like a pub is on a bar, sloppily on him. What does it matter? He could have been dead and buried by now for all I knew... he ought to be; by God, he'll be biblical soon... Anyway, what's a little inhale-exhale got to do with it? We inhale, we're momentarily alive. We exhale, we're momentarily dying. The brain gets its oxygen, the mind stays rarified. What about it?

BIG JULIE: You just recognize what we think about you.
PARSONS: I'm a skunk. I'm the sneaky wombat from The Magic Pudding.

MRS PRUFROCK: Hear, hear.

PARSONS: All right, I'll lay it on the line to him. If he's got any objections, we'll call the whole thing off. Well, we'll think about it. Okay?

> *(Grudging acceptance. SIGGIE innocently provokes him by bending over and tying up a shoelace. To SIGGIE.;*

PARSONS: Facts. First, you were born sometime in the early morning on February 29, 1831. A dead common little ugly potential, except that that year wasn't supposed to be a leap year, only your birth certificate recorded it as such.

SIGGIE: (stopping) I didn't know that.

PARSONS: Journeyed through life with your dunce's performance turned towards the wall until you left Australia January 5th, 1975.

SIGGIE: (giggles) I wanted to see...

PARSONS: (taking over) '... what the other side of the world was like'.

(SIGGIE giggles.)

'But then the war came upon me'.

(SIGGIE looks at him sharply.)

We know you've been getting quaint little nun's titters over those two dog-eared dribbles outa your mouth for years.

(pause)

And what 'war' would have that been, hmmm? Anyway, after the war you got caught up in that no one else in the world get caught up in, you ploughed over dung in a Sussex pigsty until, twenty-five years later, you were caught kissing the sow's ear.

(SIGGIE giggles again.)

Next day you were fired after calling the cows in and then forgetting to milk them.

SIGGIE: I told you I forget things.

PARSONS: (over him) So you pensioned yourself off in London and bronchitis and those foul little economies that turn all men mean. A room with grease on the walls. Crab down the stairs, jerk along London streets like an unoiled clockwork toy. Hail or sunshine, every day, you went on your round. At ten, standing in at the fruit stall, while the woman went to do her morning plough-back. She gave you fruit. At ten thirty, at the back door of the Athene restaurant. They gave you coffee. At eleven, into the newspaper office. They gave you a free paper. Read that, then over to the bakery. They gave you the leftovers which you wrapped in the newspaper. Then up to the Old People's Welfare; they gave you first scrounge over the bundles of clothing. You took something every day whether you wanted it or not. Into the library; 'Poor Mr Morrison, let him perc. on the radiator'. Counted your pennies, sniffed, simpered, faintly impertinent, sucked your teeth, until it was time for the fish shop, then the restaurant again, then to the newspaper office, back to the fruit stall... Need I go on?

SIGGIE: (sweetly) Go on; crossed paths have we?

39

(The MONOLOGUE gradually rises in volume again until eventually it fill the auditorium. The others get to their feet in somewhat alarm.)

PARSONS: (trying to keep above it) Back to the greasy room with your day's booty. When you thought nobody was looking, you used to gorby on the footpath. You crossed the road to follow a mini skirt, pretending to be looking up at the skyline while perving out of the corner of your crinkles. You wiped your hands on the wallpaper. You used to pee in the washbasin. You used to secretly fluff and secretly laugh.
    (now struggling against MONOLOGUE)
I happen to know you played with your derring- do. Really and truly you were not a very nice little man. Were you?

MONOLOGUE: (drowning him) I wish I could stare people down with my eyes. I wish I could look at people with my eyes. I wish I could look people in the eyes. Just look up and look at them. That's not much to ask. It doesn't sound much to do. Just look up and look at them in the eye. When I'm buying a chop or something and I know perhaps he's selling me a brumby and a good look in the eye would stop him from selling me a brumby, I can't give...

PARSONS: (sudden shout) Siggie Morrison, don't go back to Australia! Your sun won't shine on you again down there!

> *(Sudden cutback in sound. SIGGIE drops back onto lounge, mumbles, shivers. The others stare at each other in amazed silence.*
>
> *PARSONS is amazed with himself...)*

PARSONS: What did I just say?

JARVIS: You tell us.

PARSONS: (shouts up at control room) Testing. Testing...
    (nothing, listens)
Somebody must've left the bauble of a babble running.
    (at JARVIS)

Go up and tell the idjits to cut it out...

(As a show-stoppers, MISS GLAMORGAN appears suddenly to wander Ophelia-like, across the stage, accompanied by tragic music. She exalts the white rose she is carrying.)

MISS GLAMORGAN:
Ah, Love! Could Thou and I with Fate conspire
To grasp this Sorry Scheme of Things entire,
Would not we shatter it to bits - and then
Remould it nearer to the Heart's Desire...?
    (heavy sigh)
Oh, Sigmund...

(As she goes to float past PARSONS, he grabs her, shoves her down. She 'moons' at SIGGIE.)

MRS PRUFROCK: I wish to speak.

PARSONS: Not now.

BIG JULIE: Okay, so pay us for nothing.

(They wait again in awkward silence.)

PARSONS: (tries again, to SIGGIE) A one-armed organ-grinder, say, comes in, looks around, sees no organ-grinder and might be led to think that if there's no organ-grinder here then there might be room for a one-armed organ-grinder, even turned sideways. Not so.
    (at others)
Right?
    (They look vacuously back at him. He returns to SIGGIE)
Not being a professional that one-armed organ- grinder would be wrong. He'd be better off yanking his handle. Consider the following effect and you'll recognoitre... my amalgam and so allowed to stand... what is possible in absentia. Pavlova's dead. Brussels her next scheduled performance, but they refuse to cancel. Lights dim, last act, the dying of the swan, music up and spotlights trace the dying movements she would have made.

41

(Lights, music follow this. He holds up an arm to cease.)

PARSONS: If there's no art, there's no portence of immortality, old man. So go away and leave us professionals to render up, wafting like chantilly, whatever slight quiver-quaver might be quoited from the semiquaver from your reductible regions.

(Long pause, before.)

SIGGIE: I... think I'll have a little lie down.

(He lies back on couch, eyes closed.)

PARSONS: A damned impertinence, but an all too frequent occurrence within the confines of prosceniums, that someone walks in on the assumption that, by walking on, certain conspiracies must deliver themselves up, like rats up a drainpipe, to his requirements. Fair Muse, we can keep thee chaste, but not from being hounded.
     (pause for applause, but gets none and is hurt)
All right. He's yours. I wash my hands of him.

(Turns away.)

BIG JULIE: You've washed'n'wiped them on him. You couldn't bully a hockey ball.

PARSONS: Sitting around at a party with a zonked-out Manchester United squad sitting around you, you don't sit around looking at the wine bottle sitting there. Suggested compromise. We carry on as per schedule, and...

MRS PRUFROCK: (primly) Just a mini moment, thank you. I was trying to say before your drude indruption that either we are not wanted as yet or not wanted at all or not just plainly wanted. Not. Also, it is clear that is quite immaterial how we feel we want to be wanted or are twinned to be twanted.

PARSONS: (pained) Let's carry on rehearsing taking it from where I just left off, and if he objects just once then recuperations and aspirins on the drawing board. There he is. Scratching the surface of his mind with his pinprick of a mentality. An ideal opportunity, keeping the rag trade in mind, for us to globulize. My word and so eligible. See what happens, to you.

MRS PRUFROCK: Well, we certainly can't stand around here all night.

(They take off their coats, prepare for rehearsing, while...)

JARVIS: Day.

MRS PRUFROCK: I beg your togal ingorance.

JARVIS: Day.

MRS PRUFROCK: Night.

BIG JULIE: Day, you scarecrow.

JARVIS: (indicates SIGGIE) Ask him. That twerp was the last one in.

(JARVIS goes to move towards him.)

PARSONS: I wouldn't disturb him if I was you.

JARVIS: Who's disturbing who? He's disturbing me more than I'm disturbing him. I'll stinking disturb him if I want.

PARSONS: Let's not disturb him.

JARVIS: Why can't I disturb him? You wanted to disturb him a minute ago.

PARSONS: Put it this way. If he's disturbed enough to think he's still in England, disturbing him won't get you even the time of day. Or night.

MISS GLAMORGAN: Please don't disturb him.

JARVIS: I'll disturb the old fugger if I want to.

43

BIG JULIE: Let him sleep.

JARVIS: What's he afraid of disturbing him for?

PARSONS: Me? Afraid of disturbing that there?

JARVIS: Then what're you wetting your wraparound for?

PARSONS: Order. 'If you can't have order, you don't get served'. Practically though, he might have dropped in to die like an old bull elephant, for all I know. We've got to think of the publicity. First things: keep out hands well out of contamination range.

JARVIS: (surly) I don't like him just hanging around.

PARSONS: You're not supposed to. Scriptwise, you're supposed to despise the little shit.

JARVIS: And he looks like a little shit.

PARSONS: Of course.

JARVIS: Picking his nose, smelling it, and putting it in his mouth is enough for me.

BIG JULIE: You're nothing out of the Good Manners Guide yourself.

MISS GLAMORGAN: (blurting out) Now, you're all being rotten to him!

    (Blushes, then sulks.)

PARSONS: What's up with her?

BIG JULIE: (thumping-heart gesture) Three guesses.

MISS HOLLAND: This isn't getting us anywhere.

JARVIS: I'm going to get me somewhere. Home. Pedimobility.
    (at PARSONS)

Ever heard of that, professor? Home by pedimobility. Away from the smell of a bladder dripping out of its spout.

PARSONS: Is my suggested compromise acceptable on compromise? Yes? No?
    (JARVIS and 'BOY' vote. PARSONS slaps 'BOY's hand
    down)
You're under voting age.
    (at JARVIS)
What you can't do is simply walk away and forget him.

JARVIS: Who? Funny, I can't seem to remember who you're talking about. Bysee.

(He goes to stride off, but, arriving at the wings, unaccountably stops, unable to go further.)

PARSONS: Think of our commitments to the ghosts.

JARVIS: (sneers) Ghosts have no fannies, therefore no commitment.

PARSONS: In nineteen-o-five a John Jenkins Esquire threw himself bodily off the old balcony in The Gods, emotionally swept up in a finely-wrought melodramatic net. Mr Jenkins is just one of the many ecstatic ectoplasmics wandering hollow-eyed about us all the time. Every critic who has ever waltzed through these portals has been died in the wool. You can hear them lamenting in the wee small hours about where they spumed wrong. Suppose we left him sitting here when these our siren ghosts are stirring? We turn out the lights, leaving only a 25-watter glowing feebly off in a comer, playing giantishly with his shadow against the back projection. There are three possibilities, as I see it. One, tomorrow morning...

MRS PRUFROCK: Pardonnez-me. Tonight.

JARVIS: (now staying) Gawd. Today, today.

PARSONS: (again) One, in the hollow morrow of today, we return to find the ghost of an applause on absent ghostly pale lips and also he's defecated all over the platform of our art.

BIG JULIE: Who cares?

PARSONS: The ghosts would! Oh, let me have about me live fleshy Tribals not lean mean Caucasoids. And people would say that there's something rotten in the structure of the play. That, after more than a hundred years of whipping up the most endearing collection of improbable phantoms, all we can whip up is an old man's squirts. Two, in the hush moments of early tomorrow morning...
    (short circuits the protests)
again for the sake of argument, to someone of some seen or unseen matter, even one with a smattering of mattering, he has been left on the stage as the comment, the residue, the last murmur of our play. Yes...
    (indicates SIGGIE)
That there. The sum total. The cadaver left as art. Metaphorically, I trust you get my meaning?

    (They 'rise' to him theatrically.)

PARSONS: There. We all feeling better?
    (at MISS GLAMORGAN, 'normal')
Page twenty-seven, lovie.
    (then)
I tell you, mes enfants, phantoms relate terrible inaccuracies to each other, such that, we, as professional seekers after the underfelt, might never be able to play down.

ALL: Speak, O sage.

PARSONS: (peripatetic) Sit, my pilgrims at the fountain-head of self-preservation.

    (While they do so, duly humble, he dons a barrel, holds up a lantern.)

46

PARSONS: Show me a wise man who is not straining his resources by sitting on them. To that man I would say: leave not the little shit. To put it epigrammatically: show me the man who would leave behind a little shit uncovered and I shall show you a man who stinks.

ALL: Say on, O Wise One!

PARSONS: Consider. He who crashes in a crevasse falls on his gravity. Thus, heresayethwithal, the stage of life being darkened being cold being wet being aching with pain around the tibia region, if not around the anal region while wearing a jock strap, being truly a slimy bin even by a Pythagorean count, better to imprison him in a sunless city drain tormented by little shits until his flesh begins to rot than to leave him holed-up, incarcerated, alone, bound by art's hand-cuffs the whole night through. Who among you would face such a charge?
    (general voodoo moaning)
Take the hold-on intangible away from its teeth and a rat can be said to be a perfectly beautiful animal. Therefore, I say better draw him out like a perfectly good tooth from a rotten patient than to propagate the species.

SIGGIE: (opens his eyes) Oh, geezy's wept, it's no good.

    (They start.)

PARSONS: (at SIGGIE) Are you complaining already?

SIGGIE: Geez, no. I just can't go off. Dummy old me.
    (gets up)
God gave the tiny little birds wings to fly, not me.

PARSONS: No complaint registered.
    (snaps fingers)
Pillow.

    (MISS GLAMORGAN leaps to oblige, rests SIGGIE's head on one.)

PARSONS: Cigarette.

47

(JARVIS lights one, puts it in SIGGIE's mouth.)

SIGGIE: I don't smoke. Didn't like the draw-back.

PARSONS: Siggie old son, we all indulge the fags now and again here. All a question of function.
    (towards BIG JULIE)
Or primary urges as the case may be. Blanket! Shawl! Slippers!

(MISS GLAMORGAN fits him out, stands back maternally.)

SIGGIE: Geez.

PARSONS: Any complaints?

SIGGIE: Crikey, no.

PARSONS: Registered. Tie, collar. Handle with care.

(MISS GLAMORGAN hastens to loosen his collar.)

SIGGIE: Thank you.
    (up at MISS GLAMORGAN)
Say, haven't I seen you before?

MISS GLAMORGAN: (blushes) I'm Miss Glamorgan, Mr Morrison.

SIGGIE: Siggie.

MISS GLAMORGAN: Siggie.

SIGGIE: You know what Australians are like on first names.

MISS GLAMORGAN: Comfy now?

SIGGIE: My Miss Glamorgan died some years ago... You wouldn't have known her by any chance, wouldyer?

MISS GLAMORGAN: Partially.

SIGGIE: Partly?

48

MISS GLAMORGAN: (stroking his head) Partially.

SIGGIE: (eyes closed, purring) Did you really know her?

MISS GLAMORGAN: (affirmative) Oh, yes.

SIGGIE: (suddenly alarmed) I don't think you could've.

PARSONS: (avuncularly) That's right. Interrupt as much as you like. Locked, if you like, as we are between your side of the net and the exit.

SIGGIE: (giggles) Gawd, you gypsies. Mouths on you.

PARSONS: Consider us as more. Strange exotic friends, if you like. Close your eyes and sit back to listen to the men strumming cat-gut guitars, the women holding onto pipes and holding back moustaches, all around the campfire. Over the hillock, Toad Hall. Here...
　　　(sweeps arm)
as you rightly surmise... London airport.

SIGGIE: (suddenly indicates outside) Bloody hell... you see that? It... bounced!

(They look quizzically at each other.)

PARSONS: What bounced?

SIGGIE: That aeroplane that's just landed. It bounced. Do they all bounce like that? Stuff me, I hope mine doesn't have to bounce like that.

PARSONS: Are you objecting already?

SIGGIE: (points out) Look! That bugger of a one bounced too!

PARSONS: (reacting) Is that by way of an objection?

SIGGIE: Me, object?

PARSONS: (angry) Are you objecting to the set?

49

SIGGIE: Object?

PARSONS: Are you objecting to the sound effects?

SIGGIE: Pardon?

PARSONS: Is he objecting?

BIG JULIE: What if he is? You keep your objectionable shirt on.

PARSONS: It is no registerable objection if he objects about something I myself have already objected to. This buzzing... this orgy of Babel somebody's having with the sound track up there...
     (up at control box)
You're fired!...
     (belligerently at SIGGIE)
... that will be corrected.
     (at others)
It is not a registerable objection.

MISS GLAMORGAN: I object to you raising your voice to Mr Morrison.

PARSONS: Over-ruled.

OTHERS: (threat) Sustained.

PARSONS: Sustained.

SIGGIE: (sweetly) I read where twenty thousand. It might have been hundred... Anyway, they all fly out to Australia every year. It makes you think, doesn't it?
     (giggles)
I hope they don't try to fit too many of them onto my plane.

BIG JULIE: Isn't he a sweetie?

SIGGIE: (delighted) When I went down with my dopey old chest, I asked the doctor if I was dangerously ill and he said, no, but...
     (giggles)

I was dangerously old.

> *(Only the women laugh. SIGGIE now has the confidence to beckon 'BOY')*

SIGGIE: Little boy.

'BOY': Who, me?

SIGGIE: Come and see what Uncle Siggie's got.

> *(The 'BOY' is pushed over to him. From out of a unsavoury-looking pocket, SIGGIE produces a pear)*

SIGGIE: Would a smart looking little guy like this nice big juicy pear?

'BOY': Are you kidding? It's got after-birth on it.

SIGGIE: It's only been in Uncle Siggie's pocket. Go on.
    (forces it onto the 'BOY' who holds it gingerly.)
Would you be a dear little boy and go out and see whether Uncle Siggie's friends are waiting for him somewhere?

'BOY': Shit, try the Missing Persons Bureau, mate.

> *(And drops pear back in SIGGIE's lap.)*

SIGGIE: Your little legs are younger than my little legs.

PARSONS: Keep him sweet.

> *(The 'BOY' does a lightning tap dance. Stares back at PARSONS defiantly)*

'BOY': That's as far as I'm going.

MISS HOLLAND: It wouldn't hurt you to go out and look.

'BOY': Fucking oath it would.

PARSONS: Go out and have sniff a tin can or something.

51

'BOY': Gave that up yesterday.

PARSONS: Just as well. It's stunted your growth for the last thirty years.

SIGGIE: I'm sure if you just peeked...
 ('BOY' huffs off left)
I love little kids. They look up at you with such great big...

 ('BOY' returns from right. Walks past them all, sits.)

'BOY': Looked everywhere.

 (Accusing silence.)

PARSONS: To continue. Over the hillock, Toad Hall. Here, London airport. Someone stands. You instinctively recognize him in the pit of your stomach in the light pit of the campfire. Wolves howls turn the frost and the darkness of the night into your soul. Trinklets banging, bracelets trinkling, his voice tremoloes up from your fallen arches. He says:

 (He dons gypsy scarf, ear-rings etc. Gypsy music introduction. But this is quickly overtaken by the MONOLOGUE so that after the first few words he has to shout.)

PARSONS: ...He says: this is an ancient tale told to me by...

 (Stops. Almost immediately the MONOLOGUE subsides.)

PARSONS: ...He says: this is an ancient tale told to me by...

 (but MONOLOGUE starts up immediately to swamp him again)

MONOLOGUE: I'd expect better treatment than cats that go around doing disgusting thing anytime during the night and day like cats like you find in any old alley like you'd never find down here because even a cat doing disgusting things day and night like that need a bit of sunshine in its life even if it is night that's why Australian cats have muscles in their doo-doos.

PARSONS: (into air) Stop that!
    (listens, then)
Extrude the outside inclusions.
    (starts again)
As I was saying he says: This is an ancient tale told to me by the seventh son of a seventh son whose great great grandfather foretold the coming of the twentieth century three months before it even occurred. A true tale set in a cruel Northern Land where men eat men for the warming exercise of it all. In this land appears suddenly before all the city folk, dressed in a little pink shirt bought full four score years ago...

SIGGIE: (giggles) Like this old thing. I won it in a pub raffle in Sydney before I left and it's lasted ever since.

PARSONS: (impatiently) Like your pink one.

SIGGIE: Only this white one.

PARSONS: You had a pink one.

SIGGIE: (skeptically) It's gone a bit yellow, I expect.

PARSONS: Pink.

SIGGIE: It used to be so much whiter then.

PARSONS: (now stung) It was pink! I say so!

JARVIS: (at PARSONS) Make it white, for shit's sake.

PARSONS: No.

MISS HOLLAND: Well, it is white.

MRS PRUFROCK: As anybody can see.

MISS HOLLAND: *Now* we can see.

53

(waving script)
How do we know what else is wrong in this?

PARSONS: (stubborn) No, you don't. The three most ridiculous concepts in the world are a Jewish igloo manufacturer, a tom cat that had it winking at him and winked back, and the object of a joke in a white shirt. I absolutely refuse.

BIG JULIE: Is it white or isn't it?

PARSONS: (turns on SIGGIE) Look, are you objecting to me calling it a pink shirt.

SIGGIE: You've lost your thrilling gypsy accent.

PARSONS: Are you lodging an objection?

SIGGIE: Geez... me?

PARSONS: All right then.
      (resumes).
In a cruel Northern Land where...

> *(MONOLOGUE burst below drowns him. He 'climbs down', waits for it to subside.)*

MONOLOGUE: And what I've got a right to expect if nothing else is a bit of help from people. Someone to come up and say Siggie. Someone to come up and say my name. Just my name. That would help It's a tremendous bit of help When someone remembers your name like when they come up and say, Siggie. It's terrible when someone comes up and opens his mouth to speak but says nothing. That's terrible. That's terrible. I don't like that.

> *(Burst stops just as suddenly as it started)*

PARSONS: You will notice that despite ringing in my ears meaning I'm sickening fast, probably with a blood clot coming on, I carry on regardless.
      (restarts)

54

...dressed in a little pink shirt full four score years old, there suddenly appeared a little doll, a wondrous work of moving parts and pink little cheeks and authentic body noises as ever wormed its way around the waistbands of the wives of Man. Of its most magical movements, none was more magically moving to the wives of Man than that it talked nothing more than little nothings. Made in the image of man, it was neither woman nor man, so all the wives of Man knew it as a doll. Now being a very clever little doll, it knew the wives of Man did not want it to be anything other than a little doll, so it spoke to them in its little mechanical voice, saying: 'My, my, aren't I a clever little doll?' Hearing this, for, remember, this was a truly clever little doll, the wives of Man said to their menfolk, 'What a clever little doll!' To which all the menfolk replied, 'Pull this one; it's got bells on'. But the little doll knew full well that the menfolk of that cold, hard, cruel Northern Land had no cream in the jeans, no loving mother's milk flow for the return of the little doll to its nice sunny little cradle where it was bom, so to speak. So everywhere the little doll went, it sought out the wives of Man. And thus it was that the little doll survived, disguising itself cleverly as a little doll, for many cold, hard, cruel northern winters in that cold, hard, cruel Northern Land. And the wives of Man marvelled and clapped their hands and said, 'Truly, this is a little living doll, yeah, yeah!'

MISS HOLLAND: (bows in) Well now, one o' the Holy Father's li'l eunuchs himself, he was. A dear li'l ting, if oi may say so m'self. Oi used t'tink o' him as one o' th'lil people, with that twinkle in t'eye so he had. Every mornin' he'd tippy-toe into t'office, like, and we'd have a wee li'l chat. Oi'll always remember...

ANNOUNCEMENT: 'Attention, please. Qantas announces the departure of Flight QF 625 to Sydney, hoping to call at...'

(goes dead.

(SIGGIE strains to listen. MISS HOLLAND carries on mindless of it.)

MISS HOLLAND:... his tiny, li'l voice. Punctuated, t'was, all t'gigglin' an li'l nursery- book sayin's loik 'Glory be', meanin' praise to Himself Himself, loik, an' 'My, my'. 'My, my, what?' oi asked. 'My my oh my' said he. Sweet, loik.

ANNOUNCEMENT: 'Would passengers please disregard that last announcement'.

BIG JULIE: (stepping up to the playacting too) A girl comes across the little pixie in the bush. 'What are you?', she said. 'A pixie, what else?', he said. 'Go on,' she said. 'Let me have my way with you,' he said, 'and I'll grant you any wish you'd like'. 'Fair enough,' she said. Up he climbs, has it away, then goes to walk off. 'Hey, what about my wish, pixie?', she calls. He turns around, looks at her. 'How old are you, girlie?' 'Twenty-eight,' she answered. 'Dontcha think,' the little fellah says, 'that's a bit old to go around believing in pixies, lassie?' Old Siggie, he nearly coughed his tough little breakfast up over that. Good sport, he was.

JARVIS: (steps forward, ditto) From what I could see he had no balls.

MISS HOLLAND: I object! There was no need for that.

PARSONS: (ruling, 'in the frame') Not counted. He extemporized.

BIG JULIE: (at JARVIS) There was no need to say that.

JARVIS: I felt like saying it.

ANNOUNCEMENT: 'Qantas Airways announces the delay, repeat, the delay, of Flight QF 625 to Sydney via Athens due to Athens having gone off the map and Hong Kong. We regret any inconvenience to passengers. Please stand by for further announcements.'

SIGGIE: Oh... *blow*!

JARVIS: You got to have no equipment if all you can say when somebody tells you you've got no equipment is 'blow'. Unless you wouldn't know if a band was up you until it got drunk. Like a few here.

SIGGIE: (conversationally) The doctor told me straight. At my age I ought to be back home under the sun with my brother and sister.

PARSONS: (a martyr resisting temptation) It is not ours to disillusion with reality.

MISS HOLLAND: (knowing him) Don't you dare.

PARSONS: I didn't say a word. I stroll, I strut, I smut, I roll over on my back like a spawning spaniel but I do not... say a...
    (beginning to giggle himself)...
word... about...

    (Accusing silence. PARSONS tries to hold himself)

JARVIS: (fanning giggling) Did he say his brother and sister?

    (PARSONS is near spluttering trying to hold back outright laughter.

JARVIS: (quick glance at the script, 'performs'.) 'Ere, Siggie mate, you kept writing those flamin' letters. What 'dya expect a bloke to say? I'm on me fanny meself. Take a bit of advice. Stay where yer flamin' are. Yer too past it to travel. Stick to yer mad Pommy sheilas. Yer probably a Pom yerself now anyway. Signed, your lovin' brother, Ernie.

SIGGIE: I'm Aussie!

    (But PARSONS has broken into outright laughter, so infectiously that the others cannot help themselves either. It breaks the ice.)

PARSONS: (cueing BIG JULIE) The late and loving sister, Mrs Ethel Pot when she hears from him for the first time in forty years.

57

(BIG JULIE composes herself, steps forward, chews gum, takes gum out, sticks it behind her ear, bites her nails, hoists up a stocking , puts gum back in mouth, looks at SIGGIE mutely and bovinely, then shrugs and turns away.)

SIGGIE: (after her) I wouldn't take up much room!

PARSONS: But what would her hubby, Mr Frank Pot say? And where would they pot you? What with Frank Pot and Ethel Pot and all the little Pot tots - Peter Pot and Pollyanna Pot and Potenilla Pot and the twins, Celia and Cess Pot. Congestion, Siggie, in the Potting shed. And there's Ethel Pot's potty old pop-in-law popping in and out of the pot-hole and Frank Pot a night potter and Pollyanna working in a nights pot and Peter Pot taking pot and Ethel Pot potting her flower pots and in her pot belly another potted Pot spotted... Siggie, what a hotch-pot. Peace pots under all the beds, the whole Pot's place tottering with pots and pottering with tots, everybody taking pot luck from morning's in to night's out... I tell you, Siggie, within a week, you too would have...

(He conducts the whole cast)

ALL: Gone to pot!

(Embarrassed silence ensues, except for occasional residual snigger.)

SIGGIE: (slowly at first) I knew all along I'd finally get here. Even after somebody stole all my savings. I'm not blaming Miss Glamorgan for that. Only I would have liked to tell her I was sorry for what I used to think before she... I didn't like her... woman's smell. It's not that. But I didn't like her sugary tea with all the milk making it all cold. I didn't like to say. I didn't like the runny butter. But I never let on. She had one gold tooth and it used to shine. I wanted to tell her it didn't matter with that gold tooth she could leave the light off...

(The MONOLOGUE increases as he talks until he and it are saying the same thing, then it gradually taking over

*until he is just mouthing what it is saying and then gives up
while it carries on...)*

SIGGIE and MONOLUGUE: But what with the milk and sugar
in the tea and the biscuit I didn't like but out of courtesy I ate and
trying to watch television at the same time which I don't go on and
trying not to breathe in and trying not to look at Miss Glamorgan's
bandy legs, it was a bit much, I tell you, to take a mouthful and
then have to pull out a long strand of hair from out of my mouth.
To be straight up, it used to make me go a bit squeazy, all that
sugary tea and all... Then one arvo I was walking across the green
and there were a lot of policemen standing around her. Miss
Glamorgan, like, and they took her straight from there to the
undertaker. She looked so tucked up on that bench. I wanted to
stop. I... One day I was walking along the back lane and there was
half a cat lying by the fence. A little girl was standing over it,
looking down. If I was my sister I would have answered my
letters. I'm cold and wet. I pain somewhere.

*(MONOLOGUE subsides. SIGGIE starts to cough. MISS
GLAMORGAN flies to him, cradles him in her arms.)*

PARSONS: (quickly) Excuse me, he is emoting, not objecting.

MISS HOLLAND: Now, you've got all those beaut friends and
family back in Australia, Mr Morrison.

PARSONS: (conciliatory) Sure. For forty years, Australia's been
keeping its glass bongs crossed. From the moment you went to the
counter to buy your ticket, the word went out. Oh, yes. Through
the salons and the fin de siècle's of Europe like a dose of salts.
Galloped down the Marco Polo trail, caused the cultural revolution
in China, increased the turnover of Aussie beer in South-East Asia,
caught Borneo napping. By Darwin, the news of Siggie's returning
made the Domino Theory look like chicken feed. The whole
country went to rust-resistant seed. In Melbourne, Chloe blushed.
In Sydney, Sydney was one mass of frenzied, jerking bodies.
Anderson Department of FAT Telegraphed Requesting
Communication Urgently Telephone Melbourne 239291.

JARVIS: (taking it up) Some say the earth was feverous and did shake. The sun set its sovereign circumference on the rim of the world and, like a lover whose eyes maynst repair while others ought asleep, kept watch o'er the sweet globe of its beloved returning.

PARSONS:
Then didst the wind pummel to t'fields,
As though th'earth itself had loosed its mighty axis,
The clouds, like naked Neptune concatenated astride
His once proud trident, floundered i' the sea of Confusion's cauldron.

MISS HOLLAND: (following)
Logic, th'Mistress of Nature, did steal from its bed
And left th'house with Disorder. Some say angels
Beating aloft warriors' embellishments drove beasts
With homed heads along the Birdsville Trail...

MRS PRUFROCK:
All Nature werest o'erpotted.
Th'dogs didst railments and g-nashings at th'Masters:
Th'Masters didst derailments o'er th'Mistresses;
Th'Mistresses didst g-nashingments o'er th'Dogs;
Surf Sanderson deceased uponst 'is Board.

BIG JULIE:
The publicans went mad and lashed out free grog;
Only five dollars nonreturnable with each glog-glog-glog!

SIGGIE: (up at MISS HOLLAND) Have we met too?

MISS HOLLAND: Call me Miss Holland.

SIGGIE: How do you do?

MISS HOLLAND: Fine, thank you.

SIGGIE: I know a Miss Holland too. I think you'll like my Miss Holland. She's Irish.

60

PARSONS: (disassociating himself) Do your worst.

MISS HOLLAND: I'm sure I would.

SIGGIE: She's about the same age as you.

MISS HOLLAND: Really?

SIGGIE: Same hair, same everything.

MISS HOLLAND: What was her first name?

SIGGIE: Joan, I think.

MISS HOLLAND: Mine's Joan, too.

SIGGIE: (giggles) Ain't fact stranger than fiction?

MISS HOLLAND: (daggers at PARSONSJ Much better.

SIGGIE: She gave me this coat for a going-away thingmebob.

MISS HOLLAND: How nice.

SIGGIE: And Miss Julie gave me these shoes because they were too small for her.

BIG JULIE: I'm Miss Julie.

SIGGIE: (giggles) I thought you might be.

BIG JULIE: Sweetie.

SIGGIE: Even the old dragon herself, Mrs Prufrock, gave me a change of underps, make a man blush.

MRS PRUFROCK: (booming) I'm Mrs Prufrock.

SIGGIE: (intimately, meaning them and PARSONS) I hope I haven't upset him.

BIG JULIE: He's just here to scare away the sharks.

61

MRS PRUFROCK: (insulted at SIGGIE ignoring her) I'm Mrs Prufrock.

SIGGIE: (cringes) Hello.

MRS PRUFROCK: Somebody might have underchanged you some undies but I did. Not.

BIG JULIE: Sit down and develop.

MRS PRUFROCK: Somebody might have underpinned his underchanges, but not Mrs Profruck. Prufrock. I object to that infertience. What's more, I have said from the initial that using our own names was an invasion of privation.

PARSONS: I've told you before. Get worked up and your diction goes to the pathetic.

SIGGIE: That's it. 'Dictaphone up your diction'.

PARSONS: Dictionary.

MRS PRUFROCK: (not to be pacified) There is a dowuld of diwwerence between playing Mrs Prufrock when I am Mrs Prufruck and having a little man managing to come in... being rude here about a Mrs Purfrock, which I am not, and then dismissing me as though I was not the real Mrs Ruprock. Changing his urdies, indeed!

> *(Bored silence, except for SIGGIE trying to hold back coughing. New thought...)*

MRS PRUFROCK: Especially...
> (all sigh loudly)

Especially since if I was since his Mrs Fropuck, Propuck... oh, *shit*!

BIG JULIE: (helpful) Prufrock.

MRS PRUFROCK: Especially if I was since his Mrs Prufrock... you may not care, but happens so it does that the first Frufrocks sailed fleet first with the First Fleet... Then to call her the old dragon.

    (wagging finger)

All I can say, old little man, is that your appetite displays a great meal of inslatitude.

MISS GLAMORGAN: (has to step in) You're all being rotten to him again!

    (and begins to wail.)

BIG JULIE: (at MRS PRUFROCKJ Now look what you've done, you powdered pole.

MRS PRUFROCK: Well.

BIG JULIE: You avalanche of dishwater.

MRS PRUFROCK: Sticks and bone may break my stones.

BIG JULIE: Smarty pants. And that's a laugh.

MRS PRUFROCK: You're polluted, you are.

BIG JULIE: You couldn't buy a boyfriend on a stick.

JARVIS: Ladies, yuk-yuk.

BIG JULIE: I ain't no lady!

JARVIS: Right.

BIG JULIE: You want a black eye or something?

JARVIS: (dances around her) Come on, you underbelly of a whale.

    (They spar)

PARSONS: (renewed animation) Kick him in the crutch. Bounce off her titty and make the cancer come. More stylization. The old

Queensbury's make the best. Try John L. Sullivan. Make use of the bare knuckles.

(They stop because of his attempted choreography)

BIG JULIE: Can't anybody put the boot in without you butting in?

PARSONS: Just stay with the action!
     (grabs SIGGIE)
This hurts me more than you.

(And arranges him in a crucified position.)

MISS GLAMORGAN: Objection!

PARSONS: (ignoring her) He comes to us in supplication. Express It, cap I, for me, he asks. What do we do? We box on. We finish the last chewy. We splinter him on wood. Splinters gouging red rivers down his back. Look, his mouth falls open. Unaided, but caught up in the impetus, he moves for one apt summing up of all he has gone through, all he has ever meant to say. What comes out? An 'err' from one end and an airing from the other, then nothing. For all the freedom the umbilical becomes the mortal cord and we choke and die as purblind and bound as when we started.

SIGGIE: (but long-sufferingly) Hey, geez...

PARSONS: Quiet. Life begins and ends with the cry of a rift. Coming, the mother's when we are torn from her. Departing, our own when it is torn from us. Only one lesson in all our time. How to utter the last apt animal guttural for ourselves alone and lone. That and that alone is what is left to all of us. Listen, the rude gasps rippling the petrified forest of the material world externally.

(SIGGIE moans.)

PARSONS: One word, one succinct turn of the old verbal twirl... but grief holds him firmly by the throat. The flies of inexpressible memory are beginning to blow him.

SIGGIE: I'm aching...

PARSONS: And nobody breaks off from the championship
round to tell him we've all also clapped, very suddenly and very
loudly, in quite the wrong place at a concert. That we've all peeked
through the open blouse at the breast and will peg out haunted,
like him, by the peek-sighting of it or never knowing all the
beautiful faces we have ever seen. That the celibate who said no
man is an island was pulling our pissers. We're too near ourselves
to our own inevitable moan, thanks vee much, so...
        (SIGGIE begins coughing with the exertion)
... so when he coughs, we aim for each other's genitals. He is
already gone and lost from us, like an ice cream on roast. He
pleads silently, but we're too bored and too tired and only want to
move our own bored and tired bodies in rhythm with the St Vitus
Dance. Tell him what we can do, however, is to offer the tenacious
sinew that binds all communities of men... the privilege of arguing
the toss over his carcass.
        (casts a cloak onto the floor. Quick glance at script, then...)
So roll up, ladies and guts... suggest we read gents for guts there...
the die is cast, the dice are upcast. Page forty-three and roll it.

        (Scripts in hand, they shoot dice.)

JARVIS: (first throw) He got on my tit, but I never told him so.

PARSONS: No comment. Next.

BIG JULIE: (throws) I only tried to make him feel protected.

PARSONS: Suffocating. Next!

JARVIS: He had no balls, but I never mentioned it.

PARSONS: No opportunity. Next!

BIG JULIE: The odd bit of folding stuff thrown his way.

PARSONS: Insufficient. Next!

JARVIS: Bought him a beer when he was leaving.

65

BIG JULIE: A part-time job at my place washing up the glasses.

PARSONS: Upped! Take round one. Round two...

BIG JULIE: Mothered him.

PARSONS: Child substitution. Next!

MISS HOLLAND: (throwing) Let him sit by the library radiator every day.

PARSONS: Virtue too easy. Next!

SIGGIE: (coughing) I... can't...

PARSONS: (above him) Next!

MRS PRUFROCK: My personal attention using my fingers on him

PARSONS: Terms of employment. Cheap easy gestures. Next!

BIG JULIE: (protest) Obliged him when he wanted mothering.

PARSONS: Titty gratification. Disqualified.
     (at MISS HOLLAND)
Take round two.

MISS HOLLAND: Saved all the books he wanted.

PARSONS: Fertilizer delusions, common librarianitis. Next!

MRS PRUFROCK: Council flat, the wall-to-doors, the Wheels-on-Meals, not pooling with his fension.

PARSONS: Upped! But cancelled by typical attitudinizing.

MISS HOLLAND: Invited him to parties.

PARSONS: As Santa Claus. Self-serving. Next!

MRS PRUFROCK: Tidied up after him without saying a word.

66

PARSONS: Compounding brag with drag. But fair 'nough! Round four!

'BOY': Let him play with me down by the swings.

(SIGGIE, unable to hold position any longer, sinks to floor. As he crawls away to the couch, helped by BIG JULIE and MISS HOLLAND, MISS GLAMORGAN bursts out crying again.)

MISS GLAMORGAN: (over him) I could have looked after you so well!

PARSONS: (jumping up, 'riding her') Double seven! Pity and compassion! Can you beat that?

MISS GLAMORGAN: I could have kept him safe!

PARSONS: Oh, bowel-rending stuff!

MISS GLAMORGAN: Proper cooked meals, regular. Electric fire on all day. Tea and crumpets.

PARSONS: Score, score and score! The winner takes all!

(Holds up her hand.)

MISS GLAMORGAN: (wail) And all I did was lose his money!

PARSONS: (lets arm drop) Over-acting.

BIG JULIE: Oh, leave her alone.

MRS PRUFROCK: Well, it was idiotical in anyone's quadratic.

BIG JULIE: Who said it was, you cloistered cluster?

MRS PRUFROCK: All I was saying, keeping his money in a box under her bed. Really.

(MISS GLAMORGAN wails even louder.)

67

BIG JULIE: Don't mind them, love. They wouldn't buy grandma a walking stick if she was one-legged. Anyway, if you'd lived, you'd probably be as bald as a coot and smelling like a public dunny by now. Even old Sig wouldn't have looked at you.

MISS GLAMORGAN: He isn't well! I know he isn't well!

BIG JULIE: Corse he is. He'll live to be Australia's first man on the Moon.
    (turns on PARSONS)
All this is derivative cock.

PARSONS: Traditional.

BIG JULIE: Traditional derivative cock.

PARSONS: The derivative cock of tradition. Subessence of life.

BIG JULIE: Cock.

PARSONS: Cock subessence of life.

BIG JULIE: God, you *gliss*. My word.

PARSONS: Now you're being derivative.

BIG JULIE: And you're being bloody Jarry, Pirandello, Beckett, Saunders, Stoppard... *Their* words.

PARSONS: (dismissive) Foreigners. I'm being Commedia dell' Arte being quintessential subessential cock of the time when goat-herd man sat around on classical boulders being ponderous about the physical similarities of goats being men and men being goats.

BIG JULIE: (shaking script) Are you going to stick to this rubbish?

PARSONS: (defensive) What's wrong with it?

MISS HOLLAND: Wrong with it? After
    (indicates SIGGIE)

68

he's been here?

BIG JULIE: It's about as real as your mother's womb.

PARSONS: That's cheap and nasty.

BIG JULIE: Yeah, and so's your damn play.

MISS GLAMORGAN: (goes over to SIGGIE) I'll look after you, Mr Morrison dear.

SIGGIE: I... Kids jumping about up top, see.. *I want to go home'*.

MISS GLAMORGAN: There, there.

SIGGIE: I knew someone like you. Nice and kind. A... long time ago.

> *(Roar of another plane landing.)*

SIGGIE: There goes another one.

PARSONS: Don't tell me. Another planey-waney landing.

SIGGIE: Do they always have to bounce?

PARSONS: I bounce too. Look. Bouncey-wouncey. I'm an Indian rubber ball. What are you, some sort of rubber solution subversive?

SIGGIE: (shrinking back) I think I'll have that little shut-eye now.

> *(Closes his eyes.*

> *(Long awkward silence. JARVIS and PARSONS break it purely out of tedium. They 'throw' irrelevancies.)*

JARVIS: The aggressive confidence of a drunk staggering into a bar.

PARSONS: The staggering confidence of a woman swaggering aggressively into a bar.

JARVIS: The impertinence of someone letting you lie next to her open armpit.

PARSONS: Talking it puts the thought's nose out of joint.

JARVIS: Talking it in the pub the other night, somebody said, 'Whatcha mean I'm drunk? I'm as judger as a sob'. Then sighed like a beer keg being tapped.

PARSONS: Alternatively, the cello isn't a sexual substitute if the lady celloist is clearly seen to be losing her knee grip.

(Another silence. Nobody stirs, until MISS HOLLAND finally does so out of impatience.)

MISS HOLLAND: Oh, let's get it over with!

PARSONS (encouraged) You think so?

MISS HOLLAND: We all think so.

(and they do. MISS HOLLAND takes the lead, glances at her script, steps forward but, first, is stopped by:)

PARSONS: Just a bit.
(dashes off, returns almost immediately totally confused)
Where's everybody gone?
(nobody can help him with that)
Well, let's do it ourselves. Give's a hand.

(Between them, they pull on a bed, a few mementos on a sideboard, a door, a small section of rails denoting an outside landing, a few prison bars and a desk.

PARSONS, during this time, has pulled on an outfit resembling SIGGIE's, before going over to pull MISS GLAMORGAN away from stroking the real SIGGIE'S brow.)

70

PARSONS: You too, Florence Nightingale.

MISS GLAMORGAN: He's not well!

PARSONS: Up.

(While MISS HOLLAND delivers, BIG JULIE gets behind bars in 'gaol'; MISS GLAMORGAN, shawled and looking pale and weak, gets into bed; MRS PRUFROCK sits at the desk.)

MISS HOLLAND: Little did oi know at that stage begorrah that, loik t'laxative said, tings were cornin' to a pretty pass. There they all were wit' Fate takin' the oupper hand wit' t'help o' t'black-hearted villain Jarvis b'Jesus...

(JARVIS makes a flurried excursion onto the stage. General boos.)

MISS HOLLAND (continuing) ...stirrin' it all oup. Big Julie ratted on by th'Devil himself...
    (boos)
... picked oup, loik, when she happened t'be partakin' of an innocent stroll along t'high street at tree in t'mornin'. An' her twiggin' what was oup, but helpless, loik, in boob...

BIG JULIE: (shaking bars) Helpless! Woe that the time be arrived when having little chats with the opposite sex in the early hours of the morning on the King's highway can land you in trouble. Dobbed in by the skunk, Jarvis, I'll bet.

(Rapid tapping sounds.)

BUG JULIE: (continuing) What's that? Mice? No. Hark. Morse Code.
    (reads it)
'Help Siggie. Pension Day'. Help Siggie, pension day! Yarbles and yarsucks, something is trying to tell me Jarvis got me in here so he could stick poor Siggie up the World's End again! Well, I've still got a thingo or two up my sleeve. In particular this hammer

71

and chisel imbedded in the only outsize bulge that comes with me everytime I goes out!
(calls)
Siggie, darlin' boy, Big Jools be a-coming!

MISS HOLLAND: An' t'lilly-livered Mrs Prufrock, poxy Protestant bog, sittin' on her witherin' assets at her desk wit' complaints, loik, o' immoral practices in t'boarding house an' o' rent not paid. Complaints be Unknown Sources. ha!

(JARVIS flourishes himself on stage again to boos.)

MRS PRUFROCK: (waves letter) More complaints from Unknown Sources. It is time for me to invest a little gation.

(She gets up from desk, just as 'phone rings; picks it up, listens warily, slams receiver down and laughs awkwardly at audience. The 'phone rings again. She tries to ignore it, but has to pick it up at last.)

MRS PRUFROCK; (whisper) Not here, Commodore.
(turns her back on audience)
You know how jealously jealous Cedric jealouses. Ring me in the park instead.
(giggles)
Oh, you naughty nanny Commodore. Here.
(blows noisome kiss into 'phone)

MISS HOLLAND: An' all t'toime, Miss Glamorgan worried out o' her dear, sick moind for Mr Morrison, God love him for a saint's send-up, an' he not returned again from drawin' his pension, b'Jesus. Her on her sick bed, an' all...

(poked by a rod from the wings, MISS GLAMORGAN coughs weakly, pathetically, gazes with worried eyes at door.)

MISS HOLLAND: (continuing) The rent not paid again. Wit' Mr Morrison's savin's fast safe under t'bed. An' him not realizin' her puttin' her own money in t'li'l box for him t'be able t'go back

72

home to that Australya place an' not payin' her own rent. Loik, t'is
more'n enough t'make t'Holy Fadder Himself pity t'poor.

*(MISS GLAMORGAN strains over bed to make sure the box
is still there, lies back painfully but satisfied.)*

MISS HOLLAND: An' all t'toime, the double-dealin' devil
Jarvis...
    (general boos)
... is gettin' poor Mr Morrison t'wicked booze his pension away
again...

*(JARVIS and PARSONS, as 'SIGGIE', Come stumbling
drunkenly along the landing. PARSONS is singing Waltzing
Matilda in a piping falsetto.)*

JARVIS: You're one for the boys, skipper.
    (punches PARSONS-AS-SIGGIE in the stomach, pretending
    to be playful. PARSONS-AS-SIGGIE retches over the
    landing.)
Goodness me, don't know my own strength. Pardon oopsy-daisy.
    (general boos; cocks finger at audience)
How awfully clumsy.

PARSONS-AS-SIGGIE: Oh my oh my oh my oh my.

JARVIS: What a guy!

PARSONS-AS-SIGGIE: Oh my oh my, I think I must have spent
all my pension again.

JARVIS: (back of hand) Twenty pints of beer and fifteen shorts.
Or should I say, coloured water? Tipsy, tipsy. Half tipsy for me
and half tipsy for the barmaid. Heh, heh.

PARSONS-AS-SIGGIE: Alack-a-day, how can I return to my
sunny homeland...?

JARVIS: But you are home, skipper.
    (back of hand)

73

Home, that is, if he can pay his rent this week. Some hope. Boo hoo.

(more boos)

Tell you what, skipper, what about a little loan?

PARSONS-AS-SIGGIE: Would you? Oh, would you, Mr Jarvis?

JARVIS: (crocodile tears) If it was only up to me, I'd let you pay, say, your rent next week, but I'm only a humble rent collector. Perhaps...

(shakes head)

... no.

PARSONS-AS-SIGGIE: Oh what, Mr Jarvis?

JARVIS: Like, say, if someone found the delectable Miss Glamorgan's key lying out here, say, on the landing at, say, midnight tonight...

PARSONS-AS-SIGGIE: (recoiling) Not the fair and virtuous Miss Glamorgan's key!

JARVIS: (back of hand) Damnation! He was supposed to be shickered.

(back to PARSONS-AS-SIGGIE)

You goose, it's the only way.

PARSONS: No, no!

JARVIS: I mean to have the lovely Miss G!

BIG JULIE: Stop, you hyena's horseflesh!

JARVIS: (cups ear) What was that?

PARSONS-AS-SIGGIE: Hooray, it came from the direction of the city gaol.

BIG JULIE: You dog's fouling! You physical wreck!

JARVIS: Curses, it's Big Julie!

BIG JULIE: Flee, Siggie, love! Flee from a stinking pig who's gonna get his right up to the stinking sty when I get stinking hold of him! Fly to your homeland, Sig!

(JARVIS grabs PARSONS-AS-SIGGIE by the neck. PARSONS-AS-SIGGIE slips him, dashes to MISS GLAMORGAN'S door, struggles to open it. JARVIS lunges after him, but has his wooden leg caught in a knot hole. They both struggle individually. Touch-and-go 'chase' music. PARSONS-AS-SIGGIE gets the door open, slams it behind him.)

JARVIS: (still caught) Curses! I'll get you both for this!

MISS GLAMORGAN: (wakes up, puts out a trembling hand for him) My Mr Morrison has come back...

(and sinks back. PARSONS-AS-SIGGIE hurries over to her bedside. He coughs. She coughs. They cough together and cling to each other. General 'Aws'.)

JARVIS: (leg still caught) Don't nobody help me, will you?

(general boos)

MRS PRUFROCK: (cups ear) Hark, do I hear retuberrations on the number twenty-seven bus route?
    (she goes up to JARVIS)
Mr Jarvis, kindly your leg out of that stump take, which is blocking that knot hole and preposterating an imperticular affray all over. Town. To wit.

(JARVIS hastily unstraps his wooden leg, stands lopsidedly on stump to general delight.)

JARVIS: (ingratiating) Mrs Prufrock, lovely lady.

MRS PRUFROCK: Do you think so?

JARVIS: As I half stand here on the lopside.

MRS PRUFROCK: Enough of that, Mr Jarvis, you maughty man, you.
    (brandishes letter)
Hi 'ave complaints.

JARVIS: (confidentially) And it's about time, Mrs Prufrock, pillar of womanhood. If you see what I mean.

MRS PRUFROCK: Do you mean...?

JARVIS: Hi do.

MRS PRUFROCK: Come then, Mr Jarvis!

JARVIS: (behind her) The gravy thickens. Heh, heh.

(He waddles after her.

MRS PRUFROCK knocks imperiously on the door. MISS GLAMORGAN and PARSONS-AS-SIGGIE start, cling more firmly to each other.)

MISS GLAMORGAN: Never you fear, Mr Morrison dear. Nothing will come between you, me and the box.

MRS PRUFROCK: (unlocks the door, enters shocked) Dare I believe my eyes?

JARVIS: Go on, I dare you.

MRS PRUFROCK: So! It is true!

MISS GLAMORGAN: Oh, woe! Caught red-handed!

PARSONS-AS-SIGGIE: We'll pay all rent, Mrs Prufrock, I promise!

MRS PRUFROCK: Never mind the rent. Unless I get an expansion, I shall be forced into a verifirication that...
    (brandishes letter)
you, both of you, are immoral getters-on!

(Music. MISS GLAMORGAN sits up shocked, speechless with outrage.)

MRS PRUFROCK: Nothing to say, eh? Jarvis come then, Mr!

(And turns and leaves.

JARVIS twirls his moustache triumphantly at them, then waddles after her to boos.)

PARSONS-AS-SIGGIE: Mrs Prufrock, wait...!

(He chases after them to exit. MISS GLAMORGAN tries to follow, still trying to find words of indignation, but gets only as far as halfway across the room before...)

MISS GLAMORGAN: (to heaven)
Why should the worm intrude the maiden bud?
Or tyrant folly lurk in gentle breasts?
Unruly blasts wait on the tender spring;
The adder hisses where sweet birds sing...
    (and collapses; last gasp from floor)
Oh, sweet Mr Morrison, who will look after you now?

(On hearing her call his name, SIGGIE looks up from couch startled, sees her. Alarmed...)

SIGGIE: Miss Glamorgan!

'BOY': (emerging from under bed) Miss Julie! Miss Julie!

(And runs out.)

SIGGIE: Miss Glamorgan!
    (struggles off couch, staggers over to her)
My Miss Glamorgan!
    (and collapses beside her.)

(JARVIS returns furtively, slithers over them, steals money box and escapes.

*Over the ensuing melodrama's musical accompaniment,
sound of an ambulance siren.*

*BIG JULIE bursts out of prison, races to the rescue. She
throws open the door, sees the two bodies and stops short.
Gingerly, she rolls over SIGGIE's body. When the
realization hits her, she screams out for real.)*

BIG JULIE: *SIGGIE!*

*(including PARSONS, they all run back on stage, gasp
when they see SIGGIE.*

Blackout.

*Pale blue lighting illuminates only front few metres of the
stage.*

*Funeral music. PARSONS and JARVIS come out from left
bearing a coffin. Others follow in a bedraggled procession
across the stage.*

*The last is 'BOY'. He is followed at a distance by a
pantomime dog. The dog is stopped mid-stage. 'BOY' stops,
goes back for the dog.' He kneels down beside it, buries his
face in its neck and weeps... then gets up and leads it after
the procession.*

*MONOLOGUE rises. It continues until it fills the
auditorium and then its surrounds, carrying on throughout
the intermission.*

MONOLOGUE: And go and tell your daddies. Go and tell your
daddies or I'll tan your little bums. Go and tell a copper there's an
Aussie caught down here. Tell him I'm not Pommy. Tell him
there's an Aussie down here. The only diff was Hailey's Comet.
Tell him the only diff was Hailey's Comet. That's all the diff was.
Hailey's... what was that book? You know that book. What did that
book say? Yes. Hailey's Comet appeared during the battle in
which Attila the Hun was defeated by the Romans and the Goths.
It was also the sign in the shape of a sword which hung over

Jerusalem before the destruction of the city by Titus. It was Hailey's Comet that was pictured in the Nuremburg Chronicle for the year AD 684. If the comet's tail had been straight in nineteen-o-ten, the earth would have passed through it and this possibility gave rise to a quite remarkable excitement. People who should have known better predicted that we should be asphyxiated by poisonous gases. As it was, one or two persons were still turned in the head coinciding with exposure to the unusually large spots on the sun. Causing severe and, in some cases, permanent sun-stroke. One such case was recorded in Australia concerning an eleven-year-old boy caught outdoors. Many have regarded these people as the chosen few. There is an entirely new set of photographs in both full colour and black and white. Ideal for coffee tables. Price, five-fifty and...

(etcetera through interval).

ACT II

(MONOLOGUE gradually becomes indistinct compared to the roar of water in a storm drain.

General stage lighting takes over.

SIGGIE is laid out on airport couch. MISS GLAMORGAN is dabbing a wet cloth on his forehead. The others are sitting back watching him remorsefully. By him is a bottle of beer. The long silence is punctuated only by MISS GLAMORGAN'S whimpering.

PARSONS is about to stick a pin in SIGGIE's hand.)

PARSONS: If he objects to this, it is a cri de coeur, not a complaint.

(Sticks the pin in. SIGGIE doesn't move. Tries again, still nothing. He sticks a wooden chip up SIGGIE's nose. No reaction. Goes around, takes off one of SIGGIE's shoes, reels back. MISS GLAMORGAN screams. The others crowd around, gasp.)

JARVIS: My God, that's just got to be syphilis of the toes.

MISS HOLLAND: (with difficulty) What is it?

PARSONS: Where the water must have got at him.

BIG JULIE: What water?

PARSONS: (shrugs unconvincingly) How would I know?

BIG JULIE (Indicating PARSONS) I don't trust him.

PARSONS: If I told you, it'd only give him an unfair emotional advantage.

BIG JULIE: Something stinks around here.

JARVIS: Stink? He ought to be buried up to his knees in a cemetery.

(PARSONS overcomes repulsion to tickle the sole of SIGGIE's foot. MISS GLAMORGAN giggles. He stops. She stops. Does so again, she giggles again; stops and she stops. SIGGIE has not reacted.)

PARSONS: (at her) If he put his hand in a fire, would you?

(PARSONS walks away, sits apart. The others follow, except JARVIS who goes to take the bottle of beer.)

BIG JULIE: (catching him) Hey!

JARVIS: He won't be needing this more than me.

(But SIGGIE's hand flops over, falls proprietorially onto bottle. JARVIS has a tug of war with him, doesn't succeed and lets bottle go. He looks at SIGGIE closely, waves hand across his face but gets no reaction)

JARVIS: The little bugger's determined to take it with him anyway.

(returns to sit with others.

Long pause.)

MISS HOLLAND: I still say all that was going too far.

PARSONS: During one night in the Depression... and this was in the back stalls... they got so worked up watching Noel Coward's silver service breakfasts that three of them had coronaries before they'd even set alight to the seats.

BIG JULIE: He scared seven bells of hell out of me, keeling over like that.

MISS HOLLAND: What are we going to do?

81

BIG JULIE: We can't just leave him keeled over like that.

PARSONS: Did anyone loosen his tie? The manual says, if anyone keels over on you or... (weak laugh)... gets keeled, they say step one is you leap in and disarrange the corpus delicto around the larynx region.

BIG JULIE: That's not funny.

PARSONS: Nervousness.

BIG JULIE: You nervous? I nearly underwent my change in woman's life with him keeling over on me like that.

> *(Pause)*

MISS HOLLAND: Why doesn't somebody go out and call an ambulance? Or something.

JARVIS: At least tell them the little exhibitionist just keeled over on us.

BIG JULIE: (daggers at PARSONS) Keel-hauled, you mean.

PARSONS: What's the orangutan underbrow scowl for?

> *(BIG JULIE snaps her fingers at him. Stung, he goes to SIGGIE.)*

PARSONS: Pulse rate... thirteen in ten seconds, multiplied by six... six thirteens... that's still normal, give or take a compression or rarefaction. Heart. Like a baby's on the breast.
    (lifts arm, lets it drop)
You can't deny the limbs aren't supple, if sinewy. On the whole, not much sign of excessive, that is to say recently inflicted, rotting flesh.
    (lifts SIGGIE's eyelid)
 Eyes unrolled, merely staring mindlessly at the world. That's normal too. Respiration. Who knows how to mouth-to-mouth somebody?
    (at MRS PRUFROCK)

You've done nursing.

MRS PRUFROCK: No, thank you.

MISS GLAMORGAN: Please.

MRS PRUFROCK: I'm not lipping my pub near a near dead man.

BIG JULIE: It's just the same as kissing only you blow instead of suck.

MRS PRUFROCK: You do it.

BIG JULIE: I wouldn't want to give him my cold.

    (Long pause.)

MISS GLAMORGAN: (wail) What are we all sitting around for?

BIG JULIE: (at her) Shut up or you'll bring on my impending heart attack. By Christ, I haven't had such a scare since last week when my own body rejected my advances.

MISS GLAMORGAN:(burst) Nobody's ever given him a thought.

    (Whimpers on.)

PARSONS: Someone stop her. I'm trying to think.

MISS HOLLAND: It's too late for thinking.

PARSONS: If this got around...

MISS HOLLAND: You should have thought of that before you did this.

PARSONS: Me? We're all in together.

BIG JULIE: Who is?

JARVIS: I'm not.

MISS HOLLAND: Neither am I.

MRS PRUFROCK: I was not certainly.

PARSONS: Now if he'd had the sense to do it on the night. But this. I can't stand bad timing on stage. There is such a thing as taste.

MISS HOLLAND: Now he's blaming Mr Morrison.

PARSONS: Well, he could've keeled over anywhere in Sydney. Jesus, younger than him… they're doing it all the time. You commiserate with them about their pensions and they're liable to conk out over the counter out of sheer bloody spite. Pander to them like you were doing to him about his London lark, and it's like watching the devastation of an autumn gale on dying leaves.

MISS HOLLAND: At least he'd have died happy.

PARSONS: If he dies, he dies.

(MISS GLAMORGAN wails above him.)

PARSONS: (above her) Even dead saints only look happy because they've taken their false teeth out first. Listen.
     (shouts) '
Death annihilates.
     (again)
Death… anni-hil-ates.!
     (it reverberates)
The phonetifications… another Parsons' personal that we can and should add… alone make you shudder. Compare it to 'Tiptoe through the twilight with a tweezer just to please her'.
     (indicates SIGGIE)
Ask him. If he was alive right now…
     (MISS GLAMORGAN wails louder.)
… all right, more alive right now… he'd tell you he'd rather live for a thousand more boring years than go through the act of dying just once.

MISS GLAMORGAN: You're callous. All of you.

PARSONS: (first human reaction) You think he's got problems. I'm fifty next week.

(Turns away.)

BIG JULIE: Boo hoo. Why didn't you think of that before you done Siggie down?

PARSONS: I did not do him down. It fell to my lot to administer a certain confluence of circumstances. You say walk to an old man and he steps out in front of a car. Who do you apologise to? Circumstances are two metaphors. As delicately beautiful as a harpsichord; as solidly uncomfortable as a pew on which you're sitting listening to it.
    (MISS GLAMORGAN whimpers again. PARSONS reacts
    angrily by pushing 'BOY' off the seat)
For God's sake, take her to the powder room.

('BOY' stands his ground defiantly. PARSONS wearily takes out a packet of cigarettes, offers it to him.)

PARSONS: Here, pretend it's only tobacco.

'BOY': I don't smoke any lousy murderer's joints. C'mon, Aunt Fanny.

('BOY' exits with bedraggled MISS GLAMORGAN.;

PARSONS: Did you hear what that thing of small stunted stature called me?

BIG JULIE: It takes some crumby sort of monster.

PARSONS: He walked in here. I don't know why he did, but he did. All I know is he's been wandering around looking for some place to die from the moment he stepped off the plane in Sydney, went into a little jiggle of ecstasy at finally arriving home after forty years and got it right in the flue by the poker of the first passerby. Even I wanted to tell him that. You should've done so.

BIG JULIE: Who asked you for a speech?

85

PARSONS: (demurely) Just comes and goes.

BIG JULIE: You nearly did for me too, you assassin.

PARSONS: All this is getting nobody to the morgue.

BIG JULIE: Any more of that… just wait for me, there'll be two going.

PARSONS: If the show hadn't carried on, there would have been chaos.

BIG JULIE: Bankruptcy, you mean. For you.

PARSONS: We're actors. The set pattern; life as formal literature; you there, me here, rotate the crystal of life under the strobe, see the pretty pictures. Anyway, up yours. I'm not worried about money. My fifteen dependants are.
    (then)
It was those damn kids that found him stuck down that storm drain and didn't call for help who made it messy for us all. They should have added the coup de grace properly. But then young kids today haven't developed the grace to polish people off with any sort of *je-ne-sais-pas*. Not kids with full bellies. Bombed-out kids might. Napalmed kids, quite probably. Redfern kids with an ounce of community decency, sure. But U-beaut kids out of Banjo Patterson's land, no.

MISS HOLLAND: What kids?

PARSONS: They want to love them to death these days.

BIG JULIE: She asked you what kids.

PARSONS: Who do you know who could be so piddling as to get himself jammed down a drain on his first night back. I mean, you could drive a train through that damn storm drain and what happens… he gets discovered by some kids you could drive a toy train over.
    (impatiently)
None of you read Lost'n'Found?

86

MISS HOLLAND: (appalled) Siggie...?

(PARSONS nods, lifts SIGGIE's foot with repulsion, waves it quickly, lets it drop.)

PARSONS: Yep. Until the flesh began to rot in the storm water. Up, I believe, if you care to investigate, to at least the genital-perineum-anal straight line. A sea-green tide mark. Storm-water vintage

BIG JULIE: You *scounge*.

PARSONS: That's a repetition. I observed scientifically. I am, therefore, morally protected by diminished responsibility. No scientific observer would dare tamper with inevitability. Smoking-dash-cancer. Him-dash-Australia of forty years ago. Both show undeniables of rot-your-lungs-out.

BIG JULIE: You can damn well say what you like. Let's go, girls.

PARSONS: Fine, fine. Let's all go home. He might not be here in the morning.

JARVIS: It's already morning.

PARSONS: (exasperated) Nobody knows that until we look!

MRS PRUFROCK: (at JARVIS) I told you night not day.

JARVIS: I don't fancy coming back here in a few hours and finding him all fly-blown or something.

PARSONS: There are no flies.

JARVIS: I know a lot of flies that'd wake up just to get at him.

MISS HOLLAND: I don't understand this. You mean to say Siggie was that old man caught down that drain a few weeks ago?

PARSONS: Sad, wasn't it?

MISS HOLLAND: Knowing that didn't matter to you?

87

PARSONS: I was going to tack on a surprise ending. But that wasn't the point. The point is, the poor bugger, being tied right over the bull's-eye, something someone sometime like that would have got him right...
(uses pin to demonstrate on SIGGIE)
in the guts anyway.

MISS HOLLAND: I'm not talking about that. And stop assaulting him.!

PARSONS: He'll survive. When his little mind dribbles out of that trauma there... which I considered best to inflict for his own tooty- fruity... he'll be with us in body and soul again. He'll remember he's in Sydney. And when he walks out of here, there'll be a silent 'thank you' gurgling somewhere in his dribble.

BIG JULIE: *If* he snaps out of it.

PARSONS: (smirking) Thinking he was still in London. Seeing the set must have blown his mind into a state of thought.
(listens)
Here it comes again…

(A MONOLOGUE burst)

MONOLOGUE: : When again. the streets are white in London. When the fog is down in London. When the wind whipped up that funny smell in London. That day when I prised open a door in Soho and that big West Indian man standing there, wasn't he? Soho?, I asked him. Not bad, he said. Soho, not bad. Geez, I thought he was going to…

(stops as suddenly as it began)

PARSONS: (up at control room) I don't know what wrong with them up there. Where was I?

(But is immediately interrupted by:)

ANNOUNCEMENT: 'Qantas Airways announce with regret further delay to Flight QF 625 to Sydney via Athens and Hong

Kong that has followed Athens off the map. In any case, the captain appears to be drunk although he is a great faker and the air hostess is certainly pregnant. Thank you.'

SIGGIE: (suddenly sits bolt upright) Drat.

(The women squeal with joy, fling themselves on him, tickle him, rough his hair, etc. He writhes in delight.)

PARSONS: (joining in) Hey, you remind me of a man!

SIGGIE: What man?

PARSONS: A man of power.

SIGGIE: What power?

PARSONS: The power of Voodoo.

SIGGIE: Voodoo?

PARSONS: No, you do.

SIGGIE: What?

PARSONS: Remind me of a man.

SIGGIE: What man?

PARSONS: A man of power.

SIGGIE: (now giggling) What power?

PARSONS: The power of Voodoo.

SIGGIE: Voodoo?

PARSONS: No, you do.

SIGGIE: Whodoo?

(SIGGIE freezes as 'BOY' dashes back on, pounces on him in delight and bounces up and down on his stomach.)

'BOY': (chant) Siggie, Siggie, good old Siggie... etc.

(MONOLOGUE swells up synchronously.)

MONOLOGUE: Don't hurt my legs. Not my legs. Don't hurt my legs. Not on my legs. Get off my legs. Don't bounce up and down on my legs. Not my legs. Please not my legs. Don't. Not. Don't. Don't...

(MONOLOGUE and 'BOY' stop when SIGGIE cries out, falls back limp.)

BIG JULIE: Now look what you've done!

'BOY': What'd I do?

PARSONS: What have you been smoking out there?

'BOY': I just thought I'd jump on him a bit.

PARSONS: (simpatico) Of course you did.

MRS PRUFROCK: Well, it wasn't every clevery.

SIGGIE: (moans, opens eyes, weakly mouths at 'BOY'; finally:) Please go and tell your mummy and daddy I'm here...

(SIGGIE closes eyes. BIG JULIE motions 'BOY' off. 'BOY' obstinately shakes his head. BIG JULIE grabs him, pushes him down behind couch. SIGGIE opens his eyes again. Weakly...)

SIGGIE: (angelically) Where's that boy gone?

BIG JULIE: Gone to tell his mummy and daddy you're here.

SIGGIE: Sure?

MISS HOLLAND: Ssh.

90

SIGGIE: (closes eyes again) I think I'll...

ANNOUNCEMENT: 'Qantas Airways announces the capture of a captain who is not drunk and the air hostess has the baby standing up anyway. Please stand by for a further announcement.'

SIGGIE: (revitalized) Little bottler!

PARSONS: Panic's over, kiddies.

BIG JULIE: Panic's over, he says. I've had another two heart attacks in the last ten seconds alone.

SIGGIE: Fancy the captain being drunk and the air hostess...
    (giggles)
doing it standing up.

JARVIS: Jesus, he's come back even more demented.

MISS HOLLAND: How do you feel, Mr Morrison?

SIGGIE: It was a real deep sleep. Thank you.

PARSONS: Sleep? That was a peel-off.

SIGGIE: I was that tired and when I saw you all come back, I couldn't keep my eyes open. Dumbo me, I thought the plane would leave without me saying goodbye to you.

MISS HOLLAND: We wouldn't let you go without saying goodbye.
    (heavily)
Would we?

MRS PRUFROCK: Never.

BIG JULIE: You have a rest there before you go, lovie.

SIGGIE: I can sleep on the plane.

(They look quizzically at one another.)

91

SIGGIE: Don't they let you sleep on the plane?

MISS HOLLAND: Oh, they let you sleep on... planes all right.

SIGGIE: Don't they like you to sleep on the plane though?

BIG JULIE: You can sleep on the plane all you want, love.

SIGGIE: I'd have to have a little sleep on the plane.

MRS PRUFROCK: They love you to pleep, sleep, on the splane.

BIG JULIE: Plane.

SIGGIE: Two days on the plane without sleeping...

BIG JULIE: Don't worry. As soon as you get on the plane you sleep and don't you wake up till you reach where you want to sleep to.

SIGGIE: Sydney. Isn't it beaut?

BIG JULIE: (dully) Sydney.

SIGGIE: My father knew Kingsford-Smith.

PARSONS: (with JARVIS and 'BOY' joining in to 'Onward Christian Soldiers')
Father knew Kingsford-Smith
Kingsford-Smith knew dad
Daddy knew Kingsfordie
Kingsfordie knew my dad
Father knew Kingsford-Smith-ithie...
Kingsford-Smith knew dad... etc.

SIGGIE: I think he did anyway.
    (then)
You sure they won't mind me having a little kip out on the plane?

MISS HOLLAND: Of course not.

PARSONS: Those zoo keepers tried to kid along the Russian Panda with the British Panda and nothing came of that pandering.

BIG JULIE: (retort) If he wants to sleep on the plane to Sydney...

SIGGIE: I hope they don't mind if I snore a little. I see you've met my thrilling friend the gypsy.
   (then stiffens)
Mr Jarvis...

JARVIS: Boo!

BIG JULIE: (at JARVIS) Don't you go giving him another of his turns.

   (She holds SIGGIE's head protectively)

SIGGIE: (crushed) Miss Julie...?

BIG JULIE: What, sweetie?

SIGGIE: Could you sort of move your... I think I'm blacking out.

BIG JULIE: (hurriedly lets him go, scratching behind his ear) Better?

SIGGIE: (purring) Hmm?

BIG JULIE: Better?

SIGGIE: Uh. Down a little...

JARVIS: Would you like me to go out and buy him a dog's collar?

BIG JULIE: Nobody's asked you.

JARVIS: It's pathetic.

MRS PRUFROCK: A little humility...

PARSONS: (interjecting) A little what?

93

MRS PRUFROCK: Humbility.

PARSONS: Erase. Your word, not mine.

MRS PRUFROCK: Humbility hurts nobody.

PARSONS: Oh no? That monstrosity of a tongue trip 'humbility' is hurting me right in the sensibility.

JARVIS: And her coddling him like a teddy bear is giving me the willies.

SIGGIE: (from BIG JULIE's bosom) Oh dear, I hope Mr Jarvis hasn't come here to make trouble. Not on my last day.

BIG JULIE: (at JARVISJ Step back a little, please.

JARVIS: (shaking head) Uhuh.

SIGGIE: (suddenly) You cheated, Mr Jarvis!

JARVIS: Eh?

SIGGIE: He's stole my money!

JARVIS: I never saw his stinking money.

SIGGIE: (tugs her arm) All my savings.

JARVIS: (assumes villainy) Ah, the savings. Hee, hee. Ho, ho.

SIGGIE: (agitated) Thief!

JARVIS: (mock swoop) Whoo...

BIG JULIE: (protective) Scram.

SIGGIE: Thief, thief!

JARVIS: (another pass) Whoo...

BIG JULIE: So help me...

*(BIG JULIE levers herself up by putting her hand on
SIGGIE's head. There is a loud crack. SIGGIE goes limp,
motionless, his head at an awkward angle.)*

MISS HOLLAND: Somebody... help...

PARSONS: Trying to help him is like trying to cross upstream
after Moses went down.
    (but walks across, grabs SIGGIE's legs)
A couple of you hold his head. You to the left, me to the right.
Hold his head down more. Precipitate it. Now.
    (while they try to straighten him:)
The poor old fool's been delivering himself up like water vapour
all his life. You can't blame the kids... Try turning the other way...
What were they doing? Nothing kids don't do around a park on a
Sunday morning. Kicking, jolting, insinuating, insulting their
fleeting youth across near the race... course. Take a breather.
Throwing and toeing groin-grey... groin-grey being the
predominate posthumous primary... groin-grey twigs that look like
dogs' turds and dogs' turds that look like groin-grey twigs and not
caring one dust-off which is which... Let's get him on the floor.
    (They do so. Try again, while...)
Uh... Hold it. You come down here, I'll go up there... Australia's
little kiddies amongst the basted bark breaking bottles. Sharing
their first roll 'un made from dunny paper. Directing their
explorations at silk and cotton and elastic while heading for the
old storm drain... Stop, it's no good.
    (They stand back panting.)
... The old storm drain. Look in. What do they see?
    (points down at SIGGIE)
Lo and behold, that. As though smashed up, covered with sludge
and I-won't-say-what-else, was where he'd landed when he'd fallen
out of the sky just for them to play with. Who can blame their little
minds for filling up with... look, you try pulling your end, I'll try
pulling mine... with wondertelly wonderlandment. My word. Their
own little poppet discovery. And when it opened its liquid orbs,
what does it ask them, bloody near... no good... bloody near
drowning in wave after wave of gutter spill-over? 'Buy us a little
drinkie, kiddies.' Try twisting a bit.

95

BIG JULIE: Why don't you try?

('BOY' sneaks out from behind the couch, creeps up on bottle.)

PARSONS: The least they would have thought was he was a friendly alien from outer space. They fetch the bottle. They spar at first. Then tease a little. He 'bites' like all good fairytail pets should. They dangle, take back, dangle, take back...

(Just as the 'BOY' goes to whip bottle, SIGGIE comes alive, clutches it possessively.)

SIGGIE: Did you tell your father I was here, little boy?

('BOY' walks away in disgust)

BIG JULIE: You're going to have to cut this out, Sig. My ticker won't stand it much more.

SIGGIE: (angelic) I went off again, didn't I? Cripes, I do go off sometimes. I'm really hopeless.

BIG JULIE: (relenting) Don't worry about it.

SIGGIE: I'll be off soon and then you can all forget about a dopey old bugger, eh?

MISS HOLLAND: You don't have to leave until you're good and ready.

SIGGIE: I'll write though.
       (giggles)
When you're all freezing back here, I'll be sitting back all warm and sunny under my sun down there in Sydney...

(But then shivers violently.)

BIG JULIE: Did he make me hurt you, love?

SIGGIE: I ache... somewhere. My legs...

96

(then)
I don't want to cough!

BIG JULIE: (kindly) You cough.

JARVIS: (unkindly) Cough off.

MISS HOLLAND: You go ahead and cough.

SIGGIE: (recovers) I wouldn't like you to see what comes out when I cough. I don't want to cough because it's not nice when I cough. If you put your head against my chest, just about anywhere, you can hear... gurgling.

>*(BIG JULIE signs for them to lift him on the couch, but he goes limp when they try. They give up.)*

SIGGIE: I'll be all right though when I get home, like. It's being away from your proper home that causes it. That's what the doc said. Not having the proper rations of sunshine what you're used to as a boy. When will the plane be goin'?

>*(He closes eyes again.)*

MISS HOLLAND: If you really and truly want to go back to Sydney, the plane's sure to be going soon.

SIGGIE: Promise?

BIG JULIE: On my girl guide's black net stockings.

SIGGIE: (sits up suddenly, searches in pocket, finds ticket) As long as I've got my ticket.

>*(Closes eyes again.)*

MRS PRUFROCK: Wouldn't you be more couchable on the comf?

>*(SIGGIE shakes his head, settles down.)*

JARVIS: Don't let him go off again, for God's sake.

BIG JULIE: (cuttingly) Are you talking to us?

JARVIS: I was only...

MISS HOLLAND: (dismissive) Thank you very much.

(PARSONS, JARVIS and "BOY" draw apart. The women sit on the couch and look down protectively at SIGGIE. Long pause.)

MISS HOLLAND: (touching head(My old mum's going this way too.

BIG JULIE: Anymore of this and I'll end up the same.

MRS PRUFROCK: Anybody could.

MISS HOLLAND: It's the least we can do… humour it.

MRS PRUFROCK: Yes.

BIG JULIE: Me, I only hope a hundred yard wide, five million ton rock falls on me, phfut, before I get to this stage.

MISS HOLLAND: Mum's the same.

MRS PRUFROCK: I know what it's like to be treated as a thing.

MISS HOLLAND: Poor old thing.

BIG JULIE: What more can we do?

(Long pause.)

PARSONS: I'm beginning to feel what his Pommy friends must have gone through when they were really seeing him off. The longer they wait, the more improbable it is that the bloody plane will ever leave. When his back's turned they mouth platitudes to each other about every man having the unimpeachable right to die returning home. They don't look into each other's eyes knowing that not one of them has even bothered to tell the old boy about pipe dreams, tobacco smoke delusions. What they mean, really, is that they're impatient to get him off their hands. If he's going to go, please, Mr Ratatat, let him bloody go. And quick. It's like dandruff. He's demanded too much attendance.

(at them)

Come on, let's say it for them. For all the people he's bored to diarrhea wherever he's gone. You bore us, Siggie Morrison. Go away. Go home. Degaussitate... I insist on that standing for its sound value... levitate yourself from our wear-and-tear. Let's each of us admit it and have a good old blow-through.

BIG JULIE: (at him) You blow through.

MRS PRUFROCK: (about PARSONS) Was he parlez-vousing us?

BIG JULIE: He'd be lucky.
    (in SIGGIE's ear)
Siggie?

SIGGIE: (luxuriously) Hmmm?

BIG JULIE: (for SIGGIE's benefit, at PARSONS) Look, you fake gypsy, we've come here to see our friend here off. Now beat it.

PARSONS: I challenge that, on the grounds of over-committing your character part.

BIG JULIE: We said no fortune-telling. Go brush up on your Romany accent.

(They turn away from PARSONS. He whistles at them.)

BIG JULIE: He's hopeful.

MRS PRUFROCK: I've heard all agout bypsies.

MISS HOLLAND: (in his ear) They're shocking places for it, airports, Siggie. Pick-up merchants.

SIGGIE: (eyes still closed) Yeah, are they?

99

PARSONS: (from afar) I warn you. Beneath that pixie exterior lurks a machine tool with a diamond-hard cutting edge.

BIG JULIE: Take no notice of the nasty gypsy, Sig.

PARSONS: (at JARVIS and 'BOY') It's a joy to watch a professional at work. He's been here a... what?... microdot on Big Ben's main flywheel... and already he's polarized us into sexes. Frail, but as deceptive as transparent armoured glass between the handymen and the harem.

JARVIS: Othello without his urge tubes.

PARSONS: ('music hall') Did you just make that up?

JARVIS: (ditto) I did.

PARSONS: I say, I say, I say. I congratulate you.

JARVIS: Thank you, I say, I say.

PARSONS: I take it you have hidden talents?

JARVIS: I have hidden urges.

PARSONS: To be truthful people only laugh at me when I have a hangover.

JARVIS: (drily) Ha. Ha.

PARSONS: Thank you. Heavy night last night.

JARVIS: Don't mention it. To be truthful, women are inclined to laugh at me for my hang-down.

PARSONS: (drily) Ha. Ha.

JARVIS: Thank you. Swinging sac all night last night.

PARSONS: Was it Othello urging his tube or Hamlet urging tube or not tube?

JARVIS: It was Antony piping, 'O! thello urges lend me your Leers! The quality of Percy is not strained!

PARSONS: Of course it was too. Excuse me.

JARVIS: Heartily.

PARSONS: I had forgotten.

JARVIS: I have forgiven.

PARSONS: Say toodleloo to the nice people.

JARVIS: Toodleloo to the nice people.

SIGGIE: (sitting up) Would anyone like to share a bit of me hard-boiled goog?

BIG JULIE: Aw.

SIGGIE: (fumbling in newspaper packet) I brought it for the trip.

PARSONS: (loudly) Ha.

SIGGIE: It was fresh after it was cooked.

MISS HOLLAND: I'd like a titchy bit, Mr Morrison.

PARSONS: (at women) I warned you. You fool around with post-erection delusions, when you're not even, to be grossly frank, very good at creating hard illusions around erections, and you'll do him more harm than good.

> *(He snatches egg off SIGGIE, witheringly*
>
> *BIG JULIE tries to grab it back.)*

PARSONS: Before you smother me with your admirable mammae...
    (smirks)
hard-boiled and fresh. Well, just watch this.

(And, with flourish, cracks egg on SIGGIE's head. It dribbles over his hair. They all reel back with the rotten-egg smell.)

PARSONS: It's so fresh, it needs an ambulance.
(then)
You really think I'd waste a good egg?

SIGGIE: (miserably) It seems a bit off.

PARSONS: That's reality, Siggie. The stinking band of a rotten egg tightening around your head. I may be quoted.
     (to the disgusted looks of the others)
Cruel to be kind.

BIG JULIE: Ain't you enjoying it though?

PARSONS: (down to SIGGIE) Look, ancient chappie, I'm going to try to appeal to your sane and sanitary prehistory. Man to... well, look, it's two thousand and fifteen, give or take the last time I gave up the drink. It is not what year in the fifteen century you think it is.

(SIGGIE lies back, closes eyes, smiles angelically at the women. This provoke PARSONS further)

PARSONS: Listen, guy... you're smack in the middle of a stage set, smack in a theatre, smack in Castlereagh St, smack in Sydney, smack in the twenty-first century or what stands for it. Which is smogly snug right in Australia. If you were still in London, would you really have your lunchy-wunchy wrapped in the Sydney Morning Herald?

SIGGIE: Oh, yes.

PARSONS: (smiles, turns to others) Just notice this quick intravenous jab of reality applied as delicately as a postcoital kiss.
     (back at SIGGIE, showing him paper)
With the date of
     (looking)
Twenty o nine or whatever... ?

(looks closer, then throws paper down)
Old man, you can be maria'd for swiping things from the
newspaper library.

BIG JULIE: (grabs newspaper) Let me see.

> *(She hands it to MISS HOLLAND and MRS PRUFROCK)*

PARSONS: Are you going to believe that date's today?

> *(They stare back with animosity. PARSONS indicates
> SIGGIE.)*

PARSONS: Are you really going to believe that bundle of
complexes?

SIGGIE: (eyes open) I've still got sarneys. Anyone want a
sarney?

'BOY': (doll mimic at him) Mama, mama!

BIG JULIE: (defiantly) I would, love.

MISS HOLLAND: (ditto) Thank you, Mr Morrison.

MRS PRUFROCK: (ditto) Thank you, Mr Mossiron.

SIGGIE: I had to make 'em with marg. because marg. doesn't
bring on heart attacks like butter, does it?
    (giggles)
Scribbled on a tombstone, 'Butter got him going'.

BIG JULIE: Ain't he a little living doll?

MRS PRUFROCK: (hep) Yeah, yeah!

> *(They stop short in a realisation, which is seized upon by
> PARSONS)*

PARSONS: (flips script) Page thirty-four. 'And all the wives of
Man marvelled and clapped their hands and said, "Truly, this is a
little living doll, yeah, yeah!"'

103

(They drop the sandwiches back into SIGGIE's lap.)

SIGGIE: I thought you mightn't like the marg. Re-member the war?

PARSONS: The Crimean War?

SIGGIE: (giggles) Oh, you gypsies.

PARSONS: Kooshti bok.

SIGGIE: Pardon?

PARSONS: Freely translated from J.K. Cannonworthy' s Die Fragmente Von Zigeuner Gesohiohten using Diels and Franz reference system... for example, D.K.3BI... would come out somewhat loosely from the Romany original as, 'Dig out, ding dong!'

SIGGIE: (indicating observation window) There goes another one. Aren't airports all the go?

MISS HOLLAND: (energy gone) Don't, Siggie.

SIGGIE: No, did you see it?

BIG JULIE: All right, see what?

SIGGIE: That plane.

MISS HOLLAND: (sits upright) Now that you mention it...

SIGGIE: Don't they bounce though?

MISS HOLLAND: I thought I did see something bounce.

MRS PRUFROCK: Mai oussi.

PARSONS: Hey, no plane.

MISS HOLLAND: I distinctly heard a plane sort of bounce.

SIGGIE: (pointing) Two.

MISS HOLLAND: (agreeing) Two bouncing.

BIG JULIE: (at PARSONS) Yeah, two.

PARSONS: News helicopter, traffic, outside.

BIG JULIE: What traffic?

PARSONS: (desperately) Commuter traffic!

SIGGIE: (giggling, pointing) Three.

PARSONS: Helicopters, helicopters, some accident!

BIG JULIE: (surlily confused) Leave me alone.

SIGGIE: I know it will be a bit of a buggery of a diffo when I get
home, but I don't care. If you don't change, you die, don't you?
Look at all those butterflies doing it. That's what I think anyway.
    (pause)
The lovely summers, gawd, do they ever make up for it.
    (giggles)
I'm starting to feel all Aussie again. Did you know, when I get the
my proper sun on me back, I come up all pink like a crayfish.
Dinky-di. Oh, crayfish is Aussie for lobster. I think. Yes, and
sometimes you sell lobsters to us and sometimes we sell our crays
to you with vinegar on Then you call them lobsters and we call
them crays. Crays is short for crayfish so I call your English
lobsters crays because that's what I'm used to being Aussie.
    (pause, he gets no reaction)
I read in a book... I always forget the names of books I've always
got my nose in... anyway, crays mate when the Aussie sun is in the
zenith.
    (pointing)
That's up there. It's over there for you. There can be a lot of...
    (thickly)
Zenith-thises. Same as the Zenith-thises for crays.
    (giggles)

If you're a bit-of-a-goer cray bloke and there's a little cray sort here and another bit of a cray sort there, you can always have your zenith here, then zip over and have another zenith there.
    (giggles)
Aren't I rude?

'BOY': (doll mimic at him again) Mama, Mama!

PARSONS: (over SIGGIE, coarse whisper) The bodies are piling up. Already the vultures are consuming the corpses, gulping down the slurpy bits.

SIGGIE: (suddenly) Please... what is this place? My legs are... aching.

> *(SIGGIE shivers while trying to fight off a coughing fit. They watch him. The restrained coughing becomes infectious until they are all doing it. BIG JULIE breaks the infection.)*

BIG JULIE: (fighting off cough) It's no good. There's one part I could never maintain and that's being some sort of Maid Marian from Sherwood Forest. Can you imagine me blushing in a thicket at an English twilight? I'm sorry, Siggie love. I'm going home.

MISS HOLLAND: We can't leave him all alone.

BIG JULIE: (stopping) Hey, anybody know where my home is?

PARSONS: Tell him straight.

MISS HOLLAND: We can't.
    (at BIG JULIE)
Can we?

BIG JULIE: What am I, all of a sudden? I'm trying to go home, here…

> *(BIG JULIE steps back and steps on SIGGIE. He lies there, under her foot, looking up with eyes long-suffering.)*

106

MISS HOLLAND: Please be careful.

BIG JULIE: (jumps off him, growls) Shit! Why doesn't he get up off the floor!

MRS PRUFROCK: I'll go future further and ask...

BIG JULIE: Don't. Just... don't.
    (moves away)
I need a drink. Who's got a drink?

MISS HOLLAND: (anxiously) Siggie? Mr Morrison?

SIGGIE: (pathetically) It didn't hurt.

MISS HOLLAND: (sotto voce) We ought to straighten him out.

BIG JULIE: If you can work it out, you straighten him out.

MISS HOLLAND: We could humour him a little. At least.

BIG JULIE: Humouring him anymore is definitely out, orright?

MISS HOLLAND: You'll feel better up on the couch out of harm's way, Mr Morrison. Let's get him on the couch.

    *(The women try again to lift him, but again he goes limp.
    They give up, resume seats.)*

SIGGIE: (rolling eyes at them) This is my face here.
    (feels it)
I know I need a bit of a scrub-up, but... excuse me for asking... don't I shine through it anymore?

BIG JULIE: Don't start that again, Siggie. Please.

PARSONS: (fed up, inserts himself again) I object. I insert one formal objection into these whole proceedings. You can add it as an erratum if you wish. Either way, I maintain that it stands and in consequence allows the movement of an adjournment.
    (snapping fingers at SIGGIE)

Go away, go away, go away.

SIGGIE: (above him) *Don't I shine through it anymore?*

MONOLOGUE: (sudden burst) You don't shine down on me anymore. You ought to shine down on me some more. It's me. Look, it's me. You ought to shine down just a little bit more.

PARSONS: (up at control room) You're fired up there! And switch off before you go!

BIG JULIE: Don't you get them in a knot too.

PARSONS: I can reposition them. Even laterally. I can hoist them. I can bam them, wham them, slam them on the floor. With a bit of specialized exercise I might even be able to throw them over my shoulder like a continental soldier. But I cannot, repeat cannot, knot them.

BIG JULIE: Just don't knot them.

PARSONS: I cannot knot them.

BIG JULIE: All right, don't get them in a twist.

PARSONS: You cannot get them in a twist. They are either in a permanent state of twist or a permanent state of untwist. If you try to get them to reverse left to right or any other way they will zong back.

BIG JULIE: You've got nothing to zong.

(Strained silence.)

BIG JULIE: Sig love, we're all feeling a bit bombed out.

SIGGIE: You go on home. Don't wait for me.

MISS HOLLAND: You do understand, don't you, Mr Morrison?

SIGGIE: Now don't you go waiting for an old cripple like me. If I get lost... oh geez... where can I ask if I get lost again?

(MISS HOLLAND sighs pointedly.)

SIGGIE: No, you go. I'll just stay down here and try to think about being all warm and dry again. And...
   (calculated bathos)
all free again.
   (but this time no one bites)
You go home to your beauty families.
   (pause)
It's just that I'm a bit worried about whether I catch a plane going the wrong way. How do you know if they're coming or going? If I go the wrong way I could end up in Alaska.

(At this JARVIS jumps up.)

JARVIS: Look, cocklehead, this is a villain's cloak. Right? I now put on this cloak. I now take it off. I now strap on this wooden leg. Notice my real leg, all of it, is now bent up behind me. I now put the villain's cloak back on. Dressed as I am now, I now provoke theatrical hissing,
   (waits. Nothing. To wings:)
Hissing.
   (still nothing)
Okay, forget the hissing.. Now ineluctably, I am the transmogrified Jarvis, the villain, the dastard. I've been drinking out of mugs like you all my life. All this goes without saying now because by now everybody... and I include the five billion nine hundred million and whatnot people in the world except you... instantly recognize me. I am now about to speak. I say, 'Oops, how awfully-awfully clumsy of me. I've just peed poor old Siggie's savings up against a wall. What a shame!' Note the chuckle, the twirl of the moustache, the... toss of the villainous cloak, the belying symbol of evil's temporality in the wooden leg. I now remove the false wooden leg
   (doing so)
... the cloak... the false moustache...
   (tries to pull moustache off, but it won't come)
I... am... removing... the... false...
   (hiss to off)

Who's been fooling around? Forget the moustache, cocklehead, for the time being. Except for the stinking moustache, I am me again. Look, Jarvis, once a feeder of mother's milk.
    (then)
So , now, knucklehead, worm your way out of that.

SIGGIE: (sweetly) Geez, I've forgiven you a long time ago, Mr Jarvis.

JARVIS: Would you believe she's...
    (indicates BIG JULIE)
been approached by the Sydney City Council to clear drunks off the streets after midnight?
    (SIGGIE giggles.)
And she's...
    (indicates MISS HOLLAND)
got as much Irish blood in her as the Opera House?
    (SIGGIE giggles more)
Would you believe I was such a darling little boy I was a trustee for the South Curl Curl Cubs?

SIGGIE: (giggles to MISS HOLLAND) I never knew that man had a sense of humour.

JARVIS: Forget I spoke.
    (turns away, then remembering something else)
Miss Glamorgan.
    (prompting others)
Miss Glamorgan. Right?

SIGGIE: (agitated) Miss Glamorgan...?

BIG JULIE: Don't you go making him peg out again.

JARVIS: (shrugs) Suggestion.

MISS HOLLAND: It might work.

BIG JULIE: It'd be risky...

JARVIS: Well, you brace him up with a couple of iron leggings or something, because I'm going to get...
(nastily to SIGGIE)
Miss Glamorgan.

(And goes off.)

SIGGIE: (outburst) He's not fit to speak the name of the dead!

MISS HOLLAND: (soothing) He's gone now.

SIGGIE: (calming) I didn't ask him to come.

PARSONS: Pardon-poke, old son, you say you saw Miss Glamorgan pegged out on a bench or whatever... love of your life, right?... but what if Jarvis just happens to trot back in here with her in tow?

(SIGGIE goes obstinately silent.)

PARSONS: Just say hypothetically.

SIGGIE: Hypothetaltically.

BIG JULIE: His word.

PARSONS: (at SIGGIE) Just answer the hypostalsificating... so top that one... question. Say Jarvis trots back in here with a Miss Glamorgan alive and, I assure you, bleating. But what's more, Australian. What then, little dude?
(SIGGIE remains obstinately mute)
Nothing? It wouldn't matter? Another black out? Clunk, crash, slam, click, and the old cerebral door thunders down to complete your rhino-hide fortress again?
(still no reaction; in SIGGIE's ear)
Jupiter.

SIGGIE: (keyed) The ubeaut little radio given to me by Miss...

(stops.)

PARSONS: (nods) …Miss Glamorgan.
  (command)
Right, up on your feet, old man.

(He gets SIGGIE to his feet but with surprising gentleness.)

PARSONS: Just relax old guy. Alternatively, you may shiver whenever, wherever and however you like.
  (and proceeds, not without a show of repugnance, to strip
  SIGGIE to the waist, looking at the labels of each item of
  clothing as he goes, while:)
And I bet your father knew Samuel J. Hucker too.

SIGGIE: Who?

PARSONS: Samuel J. Hucker.

SIGGIE: Who was he?

PARSONS: Only Samuel J. Hucker of the original International Dictaphone Company of Australia.

SIGGIE: Never heard of him.

PARSONS: Didn't your father know Samuel J. Hucker?

SIGGIE: Do you mean *the* Samuel J. Hucker?

PARSONS: Who?

SIGGIE: The man who told my father a joke about dictaphones.

PARSONS: Who was he?

SIGGIE: (now giggling) He was the President of the International Dictaphone Company of Australia.

PARSONS: Not Samuel J. Hucker?

SIGGIE: Yes.

PARSONS: Not the Samuel J. Hucker who told your father the joke about dictaphones?

SIGGIE: Yes.

PARSONS: Sorry, never heard of him.

SIGGIE: My old Dad knew him.

>   *(Etcetera, until PARSONS has him stripped to his underpants, tosses his singlet down.)*

PARSONS: (triumphantly) Not one item of Pommyland clothing.

>   *(Still giggling, SIGGIE shows the women the label on his underpants. PARSONS cuts them short.)*

PARSONS: English underps are common in muck. Note the right hand half turn of the phrase. 'In muck', not 'as common as'.
>   (then)
Not even anything in the wallet either, except a lot of holes.

SIGGIE: (grabs it up) I had a fiver.

BIG JULIE: (at PARSONS) Give it back.

PARSONS: How could you, a fellow unionist, think such a thing?

SIGGIE: I had a fiver. I know I did.

PARSONS: (hopefully) Are you objecting?

SIGGIE: I... don't know.

PARSONS: If you think I lifted your fiver, then feel free to object.

SIGGIE: I don't want to be rude.

PARSONS: I demand satisfaction by you objecting. You're objecting about my abuse of your person.

113

(SIGGIE shakes his head)
Of your wallet.

BIG JULIE: Don't you object, Siggie.

PARSONS: I invoke an objection out of at least one of your goose pimples.

BIG JULIE: He's not objecting just to give you an excuse to make off with his fiver.

SIGGIE: I know I had it just now. You feel the weight, you know.

PARSONS: I'll lend him a damn fiver.

(and shoves it into SIGGIE's pocket.)

BIG JULIE: You lousy louse.

MRS PRUFROCK: How could you sloop so low?

PARSONS: It would be useless to proclaim the innocence of my rich English uncle who *(a)* still thinks I'm a minor...

BIG JULIE: Very minor.

PARSONS: Who still thinks I'm a minor and *(b)* who likes to think he is helping the 'done-under' colonial branch of the family. Useless. Poor Unc, went head first.

SIGGIE: Can I get dressed now?

PARSONS: Oh, stop complaining!

SIGGIE: (at BIG JULIE) Would you like to hear my chest going, now I'm undressed...?

JARVIS: (panic, off) *Hee-ey!*

(They all stop, watch a frantic struggle with one of the side curtains. PARSONS goes over and rescues a panic-stricken JARVIS. JARVIS grabs hold of him with relief.)

JARVIS: *Creepy... out... there.*

PARSONS: Calm down.

JARVIS: (feebly) The wind up... funny... ha, ha...

(and trips over SIGGIE's suitcase.)

SIGGIE: (jumps forward) That's my fault.

(And struggles with the weight of the case. JARVIS brutishly elbows him aside, grabs hold of case and, expecting it to be heavy, heaves. Its unexpected lightness causes him to stumble backwards and fall again. SIGGIE is appalled.)

SIGGIE: Mr Jarvis!

JARVIS: God dammit!

(And flings the suitcase off himself across the stage.)

BIG JULIE: How would you like it if I slung around all you've got in the world?

JARVIS: Bloody pretending it's got something in it.
     (SIGGIE is struggling to retrieve it)
Look at the old fool now! Falling for the oldest trick in the book.

MISS HOLLAND: You did.

BIG JULIE: Siggie love, don't try our patience anymore.

SIGGIE: (chastised) I'm sorry, Miss Julie. Uh...

BIG JULIE: Put the damn thing away. Somebody'll do themselves a damage to something none of them around here has anyway.

115

SIGGIE: (struggles to take it off to one side) Uh… if it's a bit heavy for an old codger like me, how's the plane going to go?

MISS HOLLAND: Mr Morrison, it's really empty, isn't it?

SIGGIE: I had to sit on it to get it closed.
(looks from one to another, then desperately)
Miss Julie, what would a man have an empty suitcase for?

BIG JULIE: Sig, don't call me Miss Julie anymore. It ain't my real name, orrightee? Just take it from me your suitcase's empty. Come around to my place tomorrow and I'll fill it up with all the male leftovers I've got hanging around.

(SIGGIE recoils by backing away from them, dragging his suitcase after him. JARVIS gets angry again, snatches it off him.)

JARVIS: Look, cocklehead!

(Roughly opens the case. It is empty.)

SIGGIE: No, look.

(He opens case. A few contents spill out as though it was overflowing. He has to get down on his hands and knees to retrieve them.)

SIGGIE: Please look. Somebody look. Look, Mrs Prufrock! Look, these nice warm socks you got me!

JARVIS: (exploding) Look, beans-for-brains!

(And grabs suitcase, hoists it high with one finger. Throws it down.)

SIGGIE: No, look.

(And just manages to lift it.)

JARVIS: You look.

(And lifts it, twirls it overhead, throws it down.)

SIGGIE: But look. Uh...
    (only just lifts it)
Please, look. Look, I'm going home! Look, they said, don't
worry... there's porters to do the heavy lifting, like...

JARVIS: Look, look, look!

>*(And does an aeroplane spin with suitcase. He loses control
>and it flies off to knock SIGGIE out. It finishes up on top of
>him. They gather around, look down at him)*

MISS HOLLAND: Not again.

BIG JULIE: Yep.

>*(Nobody moves to help him. Eventually PARSONS lifts one
>of his eyelids and holds it open for MISS HOLLAND.)*

PARSONS: Tell me if you can see a flicker.
    (then into SIGGIE's ear)
One, two, three, four, five... anything?

MISS HOLLAND: (shrugs) Red rivers.

PARSONS: Only signs of healthy decay... six, seven, eight, nine,
ten, eleven, twelve, thirteen...

MISS HOLLAND: Yes.

PARSONS: (leaning back) He can hear then.
    (loudly in his ear)
You can hear, can't you?
    (back at them)
Everybody has to shut down on the world at thirteen. Please hold
his eyelids open.
    (JARVIS does so)
Mr Mortified, you are looking upwards. You may genuinely be
thinking you are genuinely looking up at the genuine ceiling of a
genuine airport lounge. But, when that incontrovertible sense of

loss squats finally on your shoulder, comes home, as it were, alate for all the wind on Doomsday of your over-excited synapses, alights and sinks in its talons never again to let go until the flesh finally disgorges the skull, then one needs, dear old troglodyte, help to see through the blank blanking-off coming.

(and)

Now, Mr Morrison, if you look with your mind you'll see how a tiny transcriptase... nice word, but I shall not brood nor satisfaction show... of a tiny little pinprick called grief can confuse you about the time and the place and the whatever other dramatic unity is... Watch from the mortuary mat.

(up at flies)

Lower the New Guinea rain forest, Charlie!

(waits, but nothing

I said, the New Guinea rain forest, Chas!

(back at SIGGIE)

Replete, you'll notice, with Jap snipers.

> *(Still nothing. PARSONS strides off angrily. The others wait, eyes upwards to the flies. PARSONS returns from the other side of the stage.)*

PARSONS: (appalled) Deserted. Everybody.

BIG JULIE: Well, what are you? Crippled?

PARSONS: To be frank, I couldn't find the ropes.

BIG JULIE: Everybody's helpless around here.

> *(And strides off herself. Returns almost immediately and sits down refusing to say a word.)*

MISS HOLLAND: Well?

BIG JULIE: (shrugs) Who knows?

> *(An unattached scene cloth falls suddenly out of the air. Lands near, rolls, and totally buries SIGGIE.J*

PARSONS: It's like beating a beach ball on the head with a mallet.

(They heave it off him. SIGGIE is still pinned by the suitcase.)

SIGGIE: (but unmoving) Cripes. About this 'ere suitcase. I was never that strong. Good hearing, but.
    (then)
You've all been very kind.

(Long embarrassed pause; still, nobody moves to remove the suitcase from on top of him.)

PARSONS: (angrily) Everybody told you not to come back.

(JARVIS clips on a clerical collar, grabs MRS PRUFROCK. They act.)

JARVIS: I did, Mrs Prufrock. I said do not definitely go.

MRS PRUFROCK: More tea, vicar?

JARVIS: Mannered lady. A little more cream-of-the-squeeze, please.
    (she titters. Lewdly:)
A lot more cream-at-the-two-digit-pinch, Mrs Prufrock.

MRS PRUFROCK: O, you nawgy vicar.

JARVIS: Oodles and oodles and oodles of cream on the push-through, Mrs Prufrock. Hot oodles of oozing cream from the two big fiery furnaces, Mrs Prufrock!

MRS PRUFROCK: Oh, Vicked Wicar!

(And goes fainting away.)

JARVIS: Mrs P, Mrs P!

MRS PRUFROCK: (one eye open) Call me Ida.

JARVIS: Ida doreya, Ida! Lower 'em lewdly!

(She leaps upon him. They kiss pantomimely. She breaks away, indicates PARSONS)

MRS PRUFROCK: By Gob, there's Cedric!

JARVIS: Let him take his turn.

MRS PRUFROCK: Alack, I cannot. Not. I've been his prouse these twenty days. My vows got stuck.

JARVIS: (resumes being proper) Two lumps, Mrs P, please.

MRS PRUFROCK: Rock cake?

JARVIS: No, just a little congested; it's just the weather. But to return to the subject, Mrs P.

MRS PRUFROCK: By all salivable means, Vicar.

(She leaps upon him again.)

BIG JULIE: (joining in) Your wife and my vicar swapping spit! Cedric, come here and console me.
     (proffers neck)
Suckle me here.

PARSONS: Alas, Matilda, I cannot... I don't think there's enough suckle.

BIG JULIE: Is it...?

PARSONS: Yes...

BIG JULIE: Not...?

PARSONS: Sadly, alas...

BIG JULIE: You didn't...?

PARSONS: In the heat of the waltz, Matilda. Impetuosity and genetics undid me!

(SIGGIE suddenly sits up, claps.)

'BOY': Goody, goody, goody, Siggie's awake.

(SIGGIE does his best to hide under the suitcase. 'BOY' chants...)

'BOY': We know Siggie's there; we know where Siggie-Wiggie is!.

('BOY' begins dancing around SIGGIE. The MONOLOGUE rises. PARSONS endeavours to speak over it. 'BOY' keeps revolving, chanting. Abrupt charivari.)

MONOLOGUE: I can't stay down here. I can't stay down here anymore. I must get out of here. I don't think I can move to get out of here. If I could move I would get out of here. But I don't know whether I can move to get out of here. I think something in my legs must have gone. I think something's cracked. Something smells. I'm cold and I smell. I'm freezing. I won't take any notice of them. I'll make out I don't hear them. I'll make out I don't care whether they're here or not. I'll make out I'm dead. If I make out I'm dead, they'll get scared. If I make out I'm dead, they'll get scared and go and tell. If I make out I'm dead, they'll get scared and go and tell their mums and dads and…

'BOY': Siggie's got a dirty bottle, Siggie's got a dirty pie, Siggie's got a dirty bottle, Siggie got a dirty pie...

PARSONS: (fighting MONOLOGUE) They all said don't go. They were dead right, mate. You get off the plane, flushed, nervy. This is it, your big moment. The only trouble is the sun's in and it's pissing down raining. It's colder than in London and nobody knows you from Adam.
   (looking)
Or Eve. No brother. No Pots. Nobody. You get bowled over by street goons for your money. They get your only fiver. You are turned away from five room-and-boards; you have lost your

sister's address; your sole has come off your shoe; your brother has moved. You are tired. This, Siggie, is only your first day. After two days in the YMCA, you find lodgings. Three days after that, you trip over the lino on the stairs and twist your ankle. Back from hospital, you find your suitcase in the hall. Your pension hasn't come through. There's the hospital bill. And there's always the park bench.

MONOLOGUE: ...and or someone. If I was their age I would have gone and told someone. I want to be warm. I want to be comfy. If I could get my sun to shine through... if I could get out of here. If I could feel my legs. If they'd stop jumping on these tin sheets. If they were old enough to lift them... boy, would I fly! Would I ever! Boy, would I fly! Would I ever! Boy, would I fly! Would I ever! Listen, if I don't get out of here listen if I don't get out of here... Oh God, if I don't get out of here... Listen, if I don't get out of here...

SIGGIE: (above it all) HELP... ME!

> *(Cut-off to silence. SIGGIE starts to cough, tries to struggle to his knees.)*

PARSONS: (almost kindly) After only three months you're seventy-two years of age according to writ and just another down-and-out Aussie. Try to remember, old son. Don't you remember that day in the park when you stopped up short. The grass was brown. No little dickey birds singing anymore. All the flowers were just burnt out husks... You weren't saying shine on me, but please don't shine on me. Okay? You stalled, stopping the through traffic. You swayed like a Catholic harridan in grief. Somebody... me, I admit it... somebody heard you cry out:

> *(orchestrates for:)*

SIGGIE: (outcry) What is this place?

> *(and doubles up in another coughing fit.)*

PARSONS: (finishing off) Right. But don't overdo it.

MISS HOLLAND: (kneels by SIGGIE) Mr Morrison, we're only acting. Try to understand.

PARSONS: What she means is you're colliding with what we're colliding with. The elision collision of illusion.

MISS HOLLAND: What he means is our illusion is more powerful than your illusion, Mr Morrison, I guess. Looks like.

PARSONS: She means ours is very well rehearsed, thank you.

MISS HOLLAND: What I mean is it's in the nature of things. We've gone on over it and arrived at a something or other.

PARSONS: She is groping pathetically for the word symmetry.

MISS HOLLAND: What he's trying to so rudely say, Mr Morrison, is that we can't be what you want us to be and act and be ourselves all at the same time.

PARSONS: What she is trying to say is, our real faces are behind our masks. You can't put the faces you want onto those masks. If you could, then there would be no real faces and no real masks because there would be a real face behind the mask and a real face in front of the mask and the mask would then be just one of the real faces in between. If every mask was a real face and every face was a real mask, then there would be only one real face and only one real mask which were the same over and over again. For all of us. And only one illusion which could not be an illusion because then it would be real. And if we had no possible illusions left, old sausage old chum, we'd all go mad.

JARVIS: (jumps up) Who called me mad? When the popinjay sang 'sweet dilly dingle' to the live turkey-turtle, the dead turkey-turtle took off and registered mach three. Causing Herr Vogel to discover Herr Algol discovering the new star Mira Ceti, which he named Mata Hari. Now the repercussions were not, as Lord Lick thought, that stellar was the proper name for a star such as her, but that the naming of a new star stellar should not be a Mata Hari-type plot to immortalize the singing of 'sweet dilly dingle' by the popinjay to the live turkey-turtle.

123

MISS HOLLAND: (appeal) How do you tell him to go home?

(SIGGIE recovers enough to get to his feet.

He backs away from them, struggles to drag his suitcase with him towards the exit backstage. MISS HOLLAND pleads with him.)

MISS HOLLAND: We only want to tell you you'd be better off home.

BIG JULIE: Watchit...!

(But SIGGIE falls down through open trapdoor. A crash, then silence. They walk over and stand looking down.)

BIG JULIE: I guess he's just accident-prone.

(Pause)

JARVIS: Stopped his cough, anyway.

(Pause)

PARSONS: Australia's vital statistic for the Government's future plan for the twenty-first century, folks. He must be the first man in history whose shadow deserted him for being too dangerous to go around with. I mean, observe it, the final eucharist to the running, jumping, standing-still life. A bony residue of the overheated crucible. All of you were right. I admit it grandiloquently. One extended gaze at him should have told me he needed no literary bromide in his tea. I will renounce my masterpiece...

BIG JULIE: Great loss.

PARSONS: (theatrical) No. No recriminations. No pleas. I renounce it. I cast it into the flames, master flash drive 'n'all. It has been fouled upon by the Real Thing. Bloody impertinence. No. I renounce it.

BIG JULIE: Coming, Sig.

(And goes to climb down into the trap.)

PARSONS:... except
       (She stops.)
... except to indulge just once more, before burning the Bitch
Muse as a propitiation at the stake, pages eighty-eight and eighty-
nine, my ducks and drakes...
       (recites)
The supercilious silliness
Of this poor wingless bird
Is cosmically comic
And stellarly absurd

BIG JULIE: (resisting his 'temptation') No!

PARSONS: Please. Just once. For James McKellar who in
nineteen ninety-two martyred himself when he dashed up on the
stage just as I was on my toes to thrust down with delicate
precision the banderilla of my final line.

BIG JULIE: Definitely no.

MISS HOLLAND: Let's just carry him outside and... leave him
somewhere.

PARSONS: Please. An artist begs you.

BIG JULIE: Ha.

PARSONS: An ordinary man begs you.

BIG JULIE: (stopping) How ordinary?

PARSONS: Oh, fairly ordinary.

BIG JULIE: How ordinary?

PARSONS: Quite ordinary.

BIG JULIE: How?

125

PARSONS: Dead ordinary.

BIG JULIE: (satisfied) Let's get the damn ordinary thing over with then.

(They somewhat reluctantly don Hellenic robes. The women in strophe, while JARVIS in antistrophe.)

THE WOMEN:
He has returned
He has returned from the tempestuous journey.
O Lord Zeus, son of Cronus and Rhea,
O Arch-cynic of sisterly intercourse,
See the hero's scars, his wounds,
The weeping carbuncle of life's journey!
Set him, O Zeus, immortal amongst the firmaments!
Paste him into the vault of Heaven
As a navigational aid to the ship of life!

JARVIS: (antistrophe)
Whom do you mean by all that's indecent
In a decent Dionysian orgy?

THE WOMEN:
Oedipus Siggeus, contumelious, vessel of arrogant pride,
But beloved by a majority rule of one -- himself.

JARVIS:
Speak then of Siggie-eus, goat-herd boy; Speak, O speak of Siggie-eus!

THE WOMEN:
Who he? Who he? Who he? Who he?

JARVIS:
Pitiable wretch of human kind,
Grew up with the herd,
Stayed by the herd until he died.
Surely such tenacity deserveth rewards?

THE WOMEN:

126

Yesterday he was on the Gods' menu,
Today he is all bone and burp!

TOGETHER:
Oh, wretched little men
Make retching immortals!

SIGGIE: (manages to hoist himself up to see out) Excuse I...

PARSONS: (kneeling) Can this be a germ of an applause? The lute plucked once in singular recognition?

SIGGIE: (outcry) I don't want to die!

> *(And he grabs out at PARSONS.*

> *PARSONS has to prise SIGGIE's fingers open to stop them both from falling back into the trapdoor. SIGGIE falls back.)*

PARSONS: Now what makes you think you're going to die, old fruit?

BIG JULIE: You have.

PARSONS: (down at SIGGIE) I want you to know I deny that, Mr Morrison.

> *(Mumbles come up from trap. PARSONS motions for silence, strains to listen. Has to kneel down, head in trapdoor.)*

MISS HOLLAND: What's the poor love saying?

> *(PARSONS motions with arm behind him for silence. Finally, he gets up.)*

PARSONS: (denigratingly) Well, the official read-out of that little lot was; once upon a time Siggie dreamt he entered upon a small, hillside chapel. This was no ordinary hillside chapel. Oh, no. Because when little Siggie entered this little hillside chapel he

127

found no image upon the altar, but a wondrous flower arrangement. And there upon the altar sat a fabulous Yogi in deep meditation. Now this was no ordinary fabulous Yogi. His flesh was rotting and he coughed yellow and all over his lovely legs and lips were running sores, green with a nice sea-green gangrene. And Siggie saw that the Yogi was wearing Siggie's own face and, because his eyes were closed, Siggie knew he was not only dreaming but more especially dreaming about Siggie. And he knew that if that Yogi ever woke up and stopped dreaming about Siggie, then Siggie himself would no longer be. Now isn't that a nice nursery rhyme?

ANNOUNCEMENT: 'Qantas Airways announce the departure of Flight QF 625 to Sydney via Athens and Hong Kong which have found their ways back on at least the Qantas map. Would passengers make their way to Gate number six and have their boarding passes ready. Qantas Airways announce...'

(and fades.)

BIG JULIE: (incredulous) Did you hear what I heard?

MRS PRUFROCK: I did.

PARSONS: Don't be stupid.

SIGGIE: (struggling up) That's my plane?

ANNOUNCEMENT: 'Qantas Airways announce the departure of Flight QF 625 to Sydney...'

BIG JULIE: (accusing PARSONS) Deny that.

(They stand dumbfounded. SIGGIE starts coughing with the exertion of climbing out.)

SIGGIE: Please...

(But manages himself. He grabs his suitcase, drags it.)

SIGGIE: Which way, geez?

(And struggles frantically off.

Silence, before:)

BIG JULIE: I don't feel real.

PARSONS: Keep our sense of humour...

BIG JULIE: Come to think of it, I feel bloody unreal.

MISS HOLLAND: (indicating after SIGGIE) You don't think he really is... you know. Come to think of it, where are *we* anyway?

PARSONS: That's Siggie's line, not yours.

BIG JULIE: (at PARSONS) I thought you had a stinking gypsy's shifty stinking eyes but I never said anything.

PARSONS: We're all mates, aren't we? We trust each other, don't we?

MISS HOLLAND: My God.

PARSONS: (pointing) See?

> *(SIGGIE reappears from other side of the stage, still dragging suitcase. He comes in near exhaustion, casts about wildly, fighting back a coughing fit.)*

PARSONS: He's just trying to express finding his way out, that's all.

BIG JULIE: Never mind, poor Sig. I want to know what she said, where we are.

, SIGGIE: Geez... which... way, eh?

MISS HOLLAND: Somebody help him.

PARSONS: (at 'BOY') Go and help him.

(As 'BOY' approaches, SIGGIE screams, tugs suitcase away, and cringing away from 'BOY', exits again in greater panic.

PARSONS resumes equilibrium, takes command, heightened voice after SIGGIE.)

PARSONS: If you won't listen to us, you're dead, Siggie, old lad. You're back in Australia. All right, they left you to rot. Face up to it. They left you to rot down in that stinking hole, Siggie, and they didn't care a beanpole whether you pegged or not. Let's face it.

(SIGGIE returns from opposite side of his exit. He collapses over suitcase, goes into another coughing fit. PARSONS holds MISS HOLLAND back.)

PARSONS: You survived, Siggie. That's more than most, old tit. Show a bit of gratitude. Look, if you've got to the stage where you can't tell this... (indicates 'BOY')... forty-year-old delinquent from those silly bloody kids...

ANNOUNCEMENT: 'Would Mr Morrison, passenger on Qantas Flight QF 625, please report to Gate number six immediately while it is still on the map. Would Mr Morrison... etc.

PARSONS: (up at it) PIPE THAT DOWN!

(SIGGIE staggers off again.)

PARSONS: (after him) If it wasn't the kids, it would've been someone else, Siggie. Doll butchers have been on your lifeline ever since you dribbled milk down your mother's hard-boiled Australian breast. Prancing around like a pansy in a flower show. Dainty as a little pixie-wixie. That might have been all right in England, but here, Jesus, if you don't face it now, they'll strip the only layer of skin you've got left right off you, you poor bloody romantic sod!

(SIGGIE re-enters. He is in distress. He collapses with coughing. A spotlight suddenly shines down on him. PARSONS at 'BOY'...)

130

PARSONS: Sit on him quick before he busts something.

('BOY' does so, joggles mischievously up and down)

Forget it, Sig. It's been and gone. Look forward to the day when you slip your pajamas over your little pink shirt and with your dressing gown pulled over your shoulder, shuffle out into the midday sun to sit on the old garden seat and there, Siggie, to commit your last living gesture... fading away while kneading a greasy snot rag between ten digits of bone. So lie back and let the facts enjoy you. Give it up, Siggie!

(MISS HOLLAND screams.)

MISS HOLLAND: Blood!

('BOY' jumps away. She turns on PARSONS.)

MISS HOLLAND: Blood! That's what he's giving up!

PARSONS: Coloured syrup!

MISS HOLLAND: You bastard!

PARSONS: Biting his tongue!

ANNOUNCEMENT: 'Attention, please. This is the final call for Mr Morrison, passenger on Qantas Flight QF 625 to Sydney who has dropped off the end of the world. Would Mr Morrison report...' etc.

SIGGIE: (manages) Wanna go back home!

BIG JULIE: (into air) I want to know where the hell I am!

(SIGGIE leaves suitcase, having just enough energy to stumble off again.)

MISS HOLLAND: Stop him!

('BOY' grabs at him, only manages to tear off his underpants. SIGGIE escapes, his last vestige torn away.)

131

MISS HOLLAND: *You're all killing him!*

(The spotlight agitates round and round with increasing frequency rising to climax.)

PARSONS: (dancing around it) I'll tell you why, Siggie. Because behind that doll-face and those reveal-nothing eyes, Siggie, anybody can see you've got a scrounging cast-iron lining. Anybody can see you'd outlive us all by fifty years. We don't like that. Not a meat sandwich like you, Siggie. Already they've put an X-marks-the-spot on your head. Do you imagine, with life as it is, a life in which every lurking suspicion would be proved right if one was paranoid enough to check out how paranoid it is... do you think that life will let it rest there? Eh, Siggie? All you can do is forget for a time how tenaciously you have to rely on the inhuman circumstances to stay human. You add up the sum of all the numbers and it always comes to the Number of the Beast. Siggie? Listen, you poor sap, lie down now with the bitter-sweet melancholy of the animal inevitability of it all. It's useless. Your own father was mowed down by a life insurance van. No escape from that unnamed guilt... Ah!

(Spotlight stops stationary suddenly. He triumphantly 'catches ' it with one foot, flourishes.)

PARSONS: Ladies and gents, we have trapped for you... no, we bring you, in the latest putrous... my word, but no thanks needed... putrous-gangrenous-hue never been seen before by the naked eye, the shrewdest, the cunningest, the toughest, the outlivingest, the sweet grindingest, the leatheriest of hide, the real, the one and only indestructible but long-dead gone,.. Mr Siggie Morrison with his comb and paper!

('Effect' dies down. Silence. PARSONS finally turns to others after 'milking' the effect.)

PARSONS: There, how was that?

(They stare back mutely. PARSONS is hurt.)

PARSONS: Jesus, you're all as sour as an ulcer- bearer's belly. Anyway, even if it is beyond your appreciative faculties, that'll give you some idea of the effect we've got to get. So boost it up a bit next time. Energy. We've got to get them to really feel that...
(indicates stationary spotlight)
this is Siggie. Cornsummate the con.

MRS PRUFROCK: (triumphant) He means consummate the corn.

PARSONS: I mean what I said. We've got to get them to think Siggie's really here. When it moves, they've got to think it's Siggie moving. When Siggie, if we had somebody playing Siggie, cried or coughed his dreadful little ring out, this poor luminosity must evoke more pity because it is the absent image of Siggie. Just remember we're competing with the con of television.

(MISS GLAMORGAN enters)

PARSONS: And where might you have been?

MISS GLAMORGAN: Somewhere.

PARSONS: Don't be ridiculous. Where do you think you are?

(The sounds and shadows of technicians, stage hands etc. appear, continuing about their jobs as though everything was normal. BIG JULIE grabs one, half off.)

BIG JULIE: (desperately) Speak to me!

(Obviously get shrugged off without answer)

PARSONS: (back to normal) Right, shoes.
(gets SIGGIE's shoes and jacket etc, holds nose)
Phew. Remind me to get some pine forest into these.
(places clothing in spotlight; down at them:)
There you are, Sig. Say hellosies to the nice kind inept actors.
(back to them)
Okay, now let's go back to fundamentals. Movement first. Sway. Resonate your bums with the bathos. Psychosomatatize... my word

and eminently insertable... psychosomatatize with the pathos. Plug in...

(Voices fade out, although they continue to mime speaking and rehearsals.

Over them and the stage construction noises, the MONOLOGUE resumes.)

MONOLOGUE: And all the stars that were stars but aren't ' now. All the stars near and far. On the beach. Just before I left, I think. I think it was just before I left. It mightn't have been just before I left. Anyhow, on the beach just before I left, I wrote my name in the sand twenty-four times. Three rows of eight lots of my name. Three rows, each measuring two yards high and thirty great yard long with a dirty old piece of a real gum that must have been washed up on the beach where I wrote my name in the sand with a stick. I thought: if I'm going, I'm going to leave my name behind. Yes, sir. On the beach, I wrote my name in small writing and capital letters and shadow letters and script... I think they call it script... all sorts of different ways of writing my name in three rows all over the place thinking I'd leave my mark. Then a dirty great wave came in. A rotten great dirty great thumping great wave comes pounding in. The dirty greatest ever seen on an Aussie beach and me there with my head out, with my head up, and me there watching the stars come out standing with my feet on my name. And that wave came and woosh! That's all the thanks you get. Woosh! Washed it all away. Woosh! Washed it all away. Woosh! Washed it all away. Woosh! Washed it all away.Woosh! Washed it all away. Woosh! Washed it all away. Woosh! Washed it all…

(continuous until auditorium and foyer empty)

###

www.ingramcontent.com/pod-product-compliance
Lightning Source LLC
LaVergne TN
LVHW051643080426

835511LV00016B/2458